Andover Press

The Andover and North Andover directory, 1893-94:

A general directory of the citizens, business and streets, and other useful

information

Andover Press

The Andover and North Andover directory, 1893-94:
A general directory of the citizens, business and streets, and other useful information

ISBN/EAN: 9783337713645

Printed in Europe, USA, Canada, Australia, Japan

Cover: Foto ©ninafisch / pixelio.de

More available books at **www.hansebooks.com**

THE ANDOVER

AND

NORTH ANDOVER DIRECTORY,

1893-4.

———CONTAINING———

A General Directory of the Citizens, Business and Streets,

AND OTHER USEFUL INFORMATION.

A. B. SPARROW, COMPILER.

SPARROW & FARNSWORTH,
PUBLISHERS,
SHIRLEY VILLAGE, MASS.

Copyright 1893, by Sparrow & Farnsworth.

J. E. KEELAND,
—DEALER IN—
DOMESTIC BREAD, CAKE AND PASTRY,
—ALSO—
Choice Fruit, Confectionery, Cigars, Tobacco, etc.

First Quality ICE-CREAM and SODA.

FRESH AND SMOKED FISH, OYSTERS, CLAMS, &C.

Andover Street, Ballard Vale.

PATRICK V. JOYCE,
—DEALER IN—
Books, Stationery, Periodicals,
ETC. ALSO, A CHOICE LINE OF
CIGARS, TOBACCO,
FRUIT AND CONFECTIONERY,
SODA, ETC.
Tewksbury Street, Ballard Vale.

HENRY M. HAYWARD,
—DEALER IN—
Coal, Wood, Hay, Ice and Lumber.

ALL ORDERS FILLED AT SHORT NOTICE
—AND AT—
REASONABLE PRICES.

Yards and Residence,   **HIGH STREET, BALLARD VALE.**

CONTENTS.

Abbreviations,	5, 29
Business Directory,	87
Churches,	9
County Officers,	19
Educational,	23
Fire Department,	27
Index to Advertisers,	164
Index to Lawrence Patrons,	EE
Lodges and Societies,	13
Population of Massachusetts,	167
Post Offices,	21
Postal Rates,	21
Resident Directory,	29
Street Directory,	5
Town Officers,	17

MISS MARION R. CHANDLER,

Teacher of Piano Forte and Organ.

Residence, High Street, Andover.

THEODORE GEORGI,

PORTRAIT ARTIST.

Master of Crayon, Water Color and Pastel Portraits.

RESIDENCE,
No. 1 Washington Avenue.

BROWN'S
Andover and Boston Express.

B. B. TUTTLE, Proprietor.

Boston Offices: 34 Court Square, 77 Kingston Street and 105 Arch Street.

LEAVE ANDOVER, 7.45, 9.45 A. M., 12.15 P. M.
LEAVE BOSTON, 11.30 A. M., 3.20, 5.00 P. M.

PIANO and FURNITURE MOVING

By experienced men. General Jobbing, &c.
Baggage transferred to all parts of Andover.

THOMAS P. HARRIMAN,
HORSE and OX SHOEING
——AND——
General Blacksmith.
——ALSO——
LIGHT ✢ EXPRESS ✢ WAGONS
BUILT TO ORDER.

Carriage Repairing, &c.

PARK STREET,   *ANDOVER.*

THE ANDOVER ORCHESTRA.

(ORGANIZED 1872. INCORPORATED 1891.)

MUSIC FURNISHED for Balls, Parties, Receptions, Entertainments, Reunions,
and all occasions where
ORCHESTRAL MUSIC
is required.

O. P. CHASE, President and Manager.   Lock Box 78.
D. S. LINDSAY, Clerk.
WILLIAM SCOTT, Treasurer.
E. A. MEYERS, Leader.

M. T. WALSH,
—DEALER IN—
STOVES, ✠ RANGES,
—ETC., AND—
Manufacturer of Tin and Sheet Iron Ware.
PLUMBING & JOBBING OF ALL KINDS.

All orders receive prompt attention.

No. 8 Essex Street, Andover.

STREETS, AVENUES, ETC.

ABBREVIATIONS.—A. V., Abbot Village; A. D., Abbot District; B. D., Bailey District; B. V., Ballard Vale; C. D., Central District; F. D., Frye District; F. V., Frye Village; H. D., Holt District; N. D., North District; O. D., Osgood District; P. D., Phillips District; S. D., Scotland District; W. C. D., West Center District.

Abbot, School, across Phillips, to Boston.
Alms, Haverhill to High, F. V.
Andover, Boston road via depot to railroad bridge, B. V.
Back, from Main, across Salem, to North Andover line.
Baker's Lane, off Essex, below the railroad.
Bannister, from Andover to Ballard Vale.
Bartlett, from Park to Chapel avenue.
Boston Road, from Porter junc. Woburn to Wilmington line.
Brook, from 14 Central to Essex near depot.
Centre, from Pole hill to Andover, B. V.
Central, from Essex corner Main to railroad bridge.
Chapel Avenue, from Main to Salem.
Chester, from Lowell to Tewksbury, B. V.
Chestnut, from Central n. Brook across Main and Punchard ave.
Clinton Court, off Andover junc. Tewksbury, B. V.
Corbett, from Poor, via Owen Sullivan's, to Mt. Vernon, F. V.
Cuba, from Village to Mineral.
Downing, from Lowell opp. Frye to North Main, F. V.
Elm, from Memorial hall to North Andover line.
Essex, from Memorial hall, via depot, to the bridge.
Gardner Avenue, from Main near residence of Marcus M. Holt to South Main.

Green, from School to North Main opp. Morton.
Harding, from Main, across Railroad, to junction of High and Walnut.
Haverhill, from North Main to North Andover line, F. V.
High, from Memorial hall to North Andover line.
High, from Andover to River, B. V.
Locke, from School to Main.
Lowell, from Tewksbury, B. V.
Lowell, from North Main, by Haggett's pond, to Tewksbury line, F. V.
Main, from Memorial hall to Reading line.
Maple Avenue, from Elm to Walnut avenue.
Marland, from North Main opp. Harding to Village.
Marland, off Tewksbury at M. E. church, B. V.
Mineral, from Village to railroad bridge.
Murphy, Lowell, W. P., to Holt.
Morton (Pike), from Main across Bartlett.
North Main, from Memorial hall to Lawrence line, via Frye Village.
Oak, from Centre to Tewksbury, B. V.
Park, from Main to Punchard avenue.
Pearson, from North Main to Essex, near the depot.
Phillips, from Central to Main.
Porter, from Highland road junc. Salem to junc. Old Boston road and Woburn road, via estate of Asa Abbott.
Post Office Avenue, off Main near post office.
Poor, from Main, across Lowell, to Main, F. V.
Prospect, from Salem, via Prospect hill, to North Andover line.
Punchard Avenue, from Elm to Main, via Punchard school building.
Railroad, from School to Central.
Ridge, from Essex to School.
River, off Andover, B. V.
River, Tewksbury line to Lawrence line, via Merrimac river.
Salem, from Main to North Andover line.
Sand, off Andover near railroad, B. V.
School, from Main near Academy to depot.
South Main, from Main near Porter, via Hezekiah Jones estate, to Main.
Summer, from Elm, across Punchard avenue, to Back.
Tewksbury, from Andover opp. depot to Tewksbury line, B. V.
Union, from Main to Lawrence line, F. V.
Village, from Essex at the bridge to Lowell.
Village, from Centre to Andover, B. V.
Walnut Avenue, from High to Elm.
Washington Avenue, from Elm opp. Walnut avenue to Summer.

GEORGE PIDDINGTON,

FLORIST.

Having
Enlarged and Refitted
my
GREENHOUSES,

I am prepared to fill all orders for

Flowers, Ferns, Palms, &c.,

For Weddings, Funerals, Dinners, School and Church Decorations,
AT SHORT NOTICE.

Cut Flowers a Specialty.

Roses, Carnations, Violets, Etc.

Foot of School Street,
Near the Depot.

THOMAS E. RHODES,
—— PROPRIETOR ——

Electric ✳ Car ✳ Station,

MAIN STREET, ANDOVER.

ICE CREAM by the plate, quart or gallon.

Choice Confectionery, Soda,
Cigars, Tobacco, &c.

LUNCH ROOM
In connection.

T. E. RHODES,

TEACHER OF PIANO AND ORGAN.
PIANOS TUNED.
P. O. Box 311.   Residence, 19 North Main Street.

ANDOVER NATIONAL BANK.

ANDOVER, - MASS.

Incorporated 1826.   Reorganized 1865.

Capital, $250,000.   **Surplus, $50,000.**

Bank Hours: 9 to 12 A. M., and 2 to 3 P. M.
DISCOUNT DAY, TUESDAY.

M. T. STEVENS, President.   **MOSES FOSTER, Cashier.**

STICKNEY & HOWELL,
CONTRACTORS AND BUILDERS.

Plans & Specifications

Furnished for the Erection of Buildings of any style of Architecture.

JOBBING

Of any description will receive prompt attention.

SHOP AND RESIDENCE,
SUMMER STREET, NEAR PUNCHARD AVENUE.

CHARLES C. STICKNEY.   JOHN HOWELL.

CHURCHES.

CHRIST CHURCH (Protestant Episcopal).

Corner of Central and School streets.

Organized July 28, 1835. Incorporated April 7, 1837. Present building consecrated Jan. 4, 1887.

PRESENT RECTOR.—Rev. Frederick Palmer; residence, the Rectory, Central street.

SERVICES.—Sunday, 10.30 a. m., 4.30 p. m.; Sunday school after morning service.

SUNDAY SCHOOL.—Superintendent, the Rector; assistant superintendent, E. S. Thomas.

WARDENS.—Senior warden, H. H. Tyer; junior warden, H. J. Canfield.

SECRETARY OF VESTRY.—T. D. Thomson.

TREASURER.—J. T. Kimball.

CONGREGATIONAL CHURCH.

In connection with Phillips Academy and the Theological Seminary. Supplied by professors of the Theological Seminary. Located on Chapel avenue.

WEST CONGREGATIONAL CHURCH.

West Center District.

PRESENT PASTOR.—Rev. Frederick W. Greene.

SERVICES.—Sunday, preaching at 10.30 a. m.; evening service at 7; Sunday school, 12 m. Sunday evening services at Abbott District school house at 7 o'clock; also at Osgood District school house at 7 o'clock. Wednesday evening, prayer meeting at 7.30.

DEACONS.—N. G. Abbott, E. F. Holt, P. D. Smith, S. H. Boutwell.

CLERK.—E. F. Holt.

TREASURER.—F. S. Boutwell.

STANDING COMMITTEE.—Pastor and deacons.

ORGANIST.—Clara R. Boynton.

SUNDAY SCHOOL.—Superintendent, Edward Boutwell.

UNION CONGREGATIONAL CHURCH.

Ballard Vale.
PASTOR.—Rev. J. C. Evans.
CLERK OF THE CHURCH.—C. H. Marland.
CLERK OF THE SOCIETY.—Sherman Goodwin.
TREASURER.—Howell F. Wilson.
SERVICES.—Sunday, Preaching at 10.30 a. m.; evening service at 7. Friday evening, prayer meeting at 7.30.
SUNDAY SCHOOL.—Superintendent, Sherman Goodwin.

SOUTH CONGREGATIONAL CHURCH.

Central street.
Organized in 1711.
Pulpit supplied.
HOURS OF SERVICE.—Sunday, 10.30 a. m. and 7.15 p. m.; Sunday school, 11.45 a. m.
SUNDAY SCHOOL.—Superintendent, John Alden.
DEACONS.—George Gould, Dr. James F. Richards, Charles H. Gilbert, T. Franklin Pratt.
CLERK AND TREASURER.—George Gould.

METHODIST EPISCOPAL CHURCH.

Tewksbury street, Ballard Vale.
PRESENT PASTOR.—Rev. T. A. Hodgdon.
SERVICES.—Sunday, preaching at 10.30 a. m.; evening service at 7; Sunday school, 12 m. The Young People's League meets each alternate Thursday evening at 7.45. Ladies' Aid Society meets Wednesday afternoon at the parsonage; president, Mrs. A. M. Cummings.
TRUSTEES.—John Fallows, John Howell, William Hackett, C. H. Kibbee.
STEWARDS.—John Hallowell, John Fallows, Mrs. C. E. Walker, Mrs. John Fallows, Mrs. W. Lawrence.

BAPTIST CHURCH.

Essex street, corner of Central.
Reorganized in 1858.
Pulpit supplied at present.
SERVICES.—Sunday, preaching at 10.30 a. m.; social evening service at 7 o'clock; Sunday school at 11.45 a. m. Wednesday evening, prayer meeting at 7.30.
DEACONS.—Ballard Lovejoy, H. A. Hill.
SUNDAY SCHOOL.—Superintendent, Perley Gilbert.
WOMAN'S AID SOCIETY.—President, Mrs. Mary S. Jackson.

FREE CHRISTIAN CHURCH.

Railroad street.
PASTOR.—Rev. F. A. Wilson.
SERVICES.—Sunday, preaching at 10.30 a. m.; evening service, 7 p. m.; Sunday school, 12 m.; meeting of Y. P. S. C. E. at 6.15 p. m. Wednesday evening, prayer meeting at 7.45.
CLERK.—Herbert Goff.
TREASURER.—Mrs. J. Newton Cole.
SUNDAY SCHOOL.—Superintendent, J. Newton Cole.
CHORISTER.—Adam Lindsay.
Y. P. S. C. E.—President, Charles Baldwin.
WHATSOEVER SOCIETY.—President, Alice Coutts.
LADIES' BENEVOLENT SOCIETY.—President, Mrs. Joseph Smith.

ST. AUGUSTINE'S CHURCH (ROMAN CATHOLIC).

Located on Essex street.
PASTOR.—Rev. J. J. Ryan.
ASSISTANT PASTOR.—Rev. P. A. Lynch.
HOURS OF SERVICE.—Sunday, first mass, 8.30 a. m.; high mass, 10.30 a. m.; Sunday school, 9.30 a. m.; vespers, 3.30 p. m. Thursday evening at 8 o'clock, Young Ladies' Society; first Friday of each month, Sacred Heart Society of Jesus.

MARLAND HOUSE,

SCHOOL STREET,   *NEAR MAIN.*

WILLIAM MARLAND, Proprietor.

Limited to members of Phillips Academy.

TABLE BOARD, $3.00 TO $5.00 A WEEK.

A few Desirable Rooms to Let at Reasonable Prices.

J. P. WAKEFIELD,
—DEALER IN—
Choice Meats and Provisions.
VEGETABLES OF ALL KINDS IN THEIR SEASON.

Main Street, corner of Park, Andover, Mass.

J. E. WHITING,
(Established 1867,)
—DEALER IN—
WATCHES, ✻ CLOCKS, ✻ JEWELRY,
Spectacles and Eye-Glasses,
SILVER & PLATED WARE,
Knives, Scissors and Wallets.
FINE WATCH AND CLOCK REPAIRING.

Main Street,   *Andover, Mass.*

AMERICAN HAND LAUNDRY.
Mrs. A. M. HODGES, - - Proprietor.
Main Street, Andover.

Fine Custom Work guaranteed. Family Washings, finished, 50 cents a dozen; Rough dry, 25 cents a dozen. Large lots at a discount. Lace Curtains receive careful attention. Goods called for and delivered in any part of the town.

GEORGE E. DAVIS,
Painter & Paper Hanger.

GRAINING, KALSOMINING, WHITENING, &c.

Satisfaction guaranteed on all work.

Residence, 50 Salem Street, Andover, Mass.

LODGES AND SOCIETIES.

A. F. & A. M.
ST. MATHEW'S LODGE.

Regular communications the Monday on or before the full moon of each month, at 7.30 o'clock, in Masonic hall, Main street. W. M., John E. Smith; S. W., James Anderson; J. W., Winslow Goodwin; Treas., L. H. Eames; Sec., Charles E. Abbott, M. D.; S. D., W. H. Coleman, J. D., William Frosch; S. S., H. A. Ramsdell; J. S., E. F. Hoffman; Chap., George S. Cole; Mar., J. M. Bean; I. S., John Harris; Organist, Thomas E. Rhodes; Tyler, C. F. Mayer.

GRAND ARMY OF THE REPUBLIC.
GENERAL WILLIAM F. BARTLETT POST, No. 99.

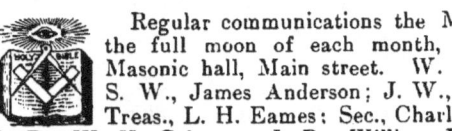

Meets the first Friday evening of each month in G. A. R. hall, Essex street. Commander, George Dane; Senior Vice Commander, George F. Holt; Junior Vice Commander, Jonathan M. Bean; Chaplain, Peter D. Smith; Officer of the Day, Henry C. Higgins; Officer of the Guard, Joseph T. Robbins; Quartermaster, Brainard Cummings; Quartermaster Sergeant, George W. Chandler; Adjutant, Charles Greene; Sergt. Major, J. Warren Berry; Surgeon, Charles H. Flint.

W. F. BARTLETT RELIEF CORPS, No. 127.

Meets first and third Tuesday evenings of each month in G. A. R. hall, Essex street. Pres., Mrs. Hannah S. Greene; S. V. Pres., Miss Jessie F. Greene; J. V. Pres., Mrs. Lizzie P. Morse; Sec., Mrs. Nellie L. Penny; Treas., Mrs. Phebe L. Coleman; Chap., Mrs. Mary A. Davis; Con., Mrs. Fannie N. Findley; Guard, Miss Elizabeth M. Buchan; Asst. Con., Miss Sadie M. Hobbs; Asst. Guard, Miss Helen Watson.

WALTER L. RAYMOND CAMP, No. 111, S. V.

Meets first and third Monday of each month in G. A. R. hall, Essex street. Captain, Frank P. Higgins; 1st Lieutenant, George W. Buchan; 2d Lieutenant, James Kibbee; 1st Sergeant, James Lindsay; Quartermaster Sergeant, Ira Buxton.

MEMORIAL HALL LIBRARY AND READING ROOM.

Elm square. Founded in 1872.

The present Board of Trustees—Joseph W. Smith, Francis H. Johnson, George W. Foster, E. Kendall Jenkins, James B. Smith, C. C. Carpenter; Joseph A. Smart, Secretary.

The Library contains about 14,000 volumes, and is open for the delivery of books each week day (except Wednesdays) from 3 to 5 and 6.30 to 9 p. m. The reading room is open from 8.30 a. m. to 12 m., and from 3 to 5 and 6.30 to 9 p. m.; Wednesday, from 8.30 to 10 a. m. and from 6.30 to 9 p. m. Ballard Holt, Librarian; J. O. Bradshaw, Assistant Librarian.

ROYAL ARCANUM.

ANDOVER COUNCIL, No. 65.

Meets second and fourth Friday evenings of each month in A. O. U. W. hall, Main street. Regent, Barnett Rogers; Vice Regent, Moses L. Farnham; Past Regent, Charles W. Clark; Orator, Louis Dahl; Chaplain, J. Warren Berry; Secretary, F. P. Berry; Collector, William B. Cheever; Treasurer, C. B. Jenkins; Guide, George E. Holt; Warden, Thomas H. Bentley; Sentry, L. C. Young.

INDIAN RIDGE COUNCIL.

Meets first and third Wednesday evening of each month in A. O. U. W. hall, Main street. Regent, J. J. Sweeney; Vice Regent, Charles Donovan; Past Regent, J. M. Bradley. Orator, William P. Reagan; Guide, A. A. O'Connell; Warden, James Nolan; Sentry, Patrick Daly; Treasurer, Roderick McIsaac; Collector, William Doherty.

ELM CLUB.

Meets first Monday of each month in Elm Club room, Main street. President, George W. Foster; Vice President, William Odlin; Secretary, George A. Higgins; Treasurer, George F. Cheever; Directors—Officers of the Club and John H. Campion, J. M. Bradley, John P. Wakefield, Andrew McTernen, C. A. Sullivan.

PATRONS OF HUSBANDRY.
ANDOVER GRANGE, No. 183.

Meets second and fourth Tuesday evenings of each month from November to May; remainder of the year, fourth Tuesday evenings in vestry of West Congregational church. Master, E. W. Burtt; Overseer, Milo H. Gould; Lecturer, Miss Clara A. Putnam; Steward, E. W. Boutwell, Assistant Steward, C. L. Bailey; Chaplain, S. H. Boutwell; Treasurer, E. F. Abbott; Secretary, Miss Angie M. Burtt; Gate Keeper, William J. Clark; Pomona, Miss May B. Hardy; Ceres, Mrs. Walter Hayward; Flora, Miss Laura J. Lovejoy; Lady Assistant Steward, Mrs. Fannie Fitz.

ANDOVER WHEELMEN.

Meet Friday evenings. President, George D. Pettee; Vice President, O. P. Chase; Secretary, Peter Smith; Captain, H. P. Chase.

SHAWSHEEN CLUB.

Organized September, 1889. Annual meeting, first Monday of January. Club room, Carter's block, Main street. President, John H. Flint; Vice President, John L. Smith; Secretary, George W. Foster; Treasurer, Frank E. Gleason.

Y. L. P. U., B. V.

Organized in 1888. Meets first Saturday of each month in Y. L. P. U. hall. President, Daniel H. Poor; Vice President, Sherman Goodwin; Secretary, Robert Ewing; Treasurer, Northy Marland.

COSMOPOLITAN SINGING SOCIETY, B. V.

Incorporated Feb. 10, 1890. Meets second Tuesday of each month in C. S. S. hall at 8 p. m. President, William Frosch; Vice President, E. F. Hoffman; Secretary, John Hax; Treasurer, Jacob Klisserath; General Agent, Henry M. Riebe.

In connection with and under the supervision of the society there is a German school every Saturday from 2.30 to 5.30 p. m. (Americans admitted.) Number of pupils, 15. President, William Frosch; Vice President, Herman F. Nehr; Secretary, Philip Noessel; Treasurer, Charles Fischer.

ANCIENT ORDER UNITED WORKMEN.
LINCOLN LODGE, No. 78.

Meets second and fourth Monday of each month in A. O. U. W. hall, Main street. Master Workman, Alexander Dick; Foreman, James Grosvenor; Overseer, Simeon Wrigley; P. M. Workman, Frederick Hulme; Recorder, E. E. Trefry; Financier, Ira O. Gray; Receiver, T. E. Rhodes; Guide, William Angus; Inside Watchman, John H. Mathews; Outside Watchman, George Higginbottom.

HARMONY ASSOCIATION, B. V.

Regular meetings first Tuesday of each month in Old School building. President, C. H. Shattuck, Jr.; Vice President, H. P. Ladd; Secretary, William S. Clemons; Treasurer, J. W. Murray.

COLUMBUS CLUB, B. V.

Meets first Tuesday of each month in Old School building. President, M. H. Riley; Vice President, Owen F. Caffery; Treasurer, William J. O'Donnell; Secretary, Hugh F. O'Donnell.

H. F. CHASE,
Machinist
—AND—
Dealer in Guns, Revolvers & Ammunition.
GUNS FOR SALE AND TO LET.
Agent for Columbia and Victor Bicycles.

Bicycles Bought, for Sale, to Let, Repaired, Stored and Crated.

POST-OFFICE AVENUE.

TOWN OFFICERS.

BOARD OF SELECTMEN.—Arthur Bliss, John S. Stark, Samuel H. Boutwell.
TOWN CLERK.—Abraham Marland.
TOWN TREASURER.—George A. Parker.
CLERK OF SELECTMEN.—Abraham Marland.
COLLECTOR OF TAXES.—Abraham Marland.
ASSESSORS.—The Selectmen.
AUDITORS.—J. M. Bradley, L. T. Hardy, Louis A. Dame.
OVERSEERS OF THE POOR.—The Selectmen.
SUPERINTENDENT OF ALMSHOUSE.—George L. Burnham.
WATER COMMISSIONERS.—John H. Flint, Felix G. Haynes, James P. Butterfield.
SUPERINTENDENT OF WATER WORKS.—John E. Smith.
COLLECTOR OF WATER RATES.—Fred A. Andrews.
CONSTABLES.—George F. Cheever, Elmer H. Shattuck, Barnett Rogers.
CHIEF OF POLICE.—George F. Cheever.
SUPERINTENDENT OF STREETS.—Joseph T. Lovejoy.
TOWN PHYSICIAN.—Charles E. Abbott, M. D.
BOARD OF REGISTRATION.—Henry McLawlin, Joseph F. Cole, Charles A. H. Fischer, Abraham Marland.
BOARD OF HEALTH.—George S. Cole, Howell F. Wilson, Dr. C. E. Abbott.

REPUBLICAN TOWN COMMITTEE.

George S. Cole, Chairman; O. P. Chase, Secretary and Treasurer; C. H. Shattuck, Jr., Fred M. Hill, Harry A. Ramsdell.

DEMOCRATIC TOWN COMMITTEE.

John J. Sweeney, Chairman; E. E. Trefry, Secretary; Joseph M. Bradley, Michael T. Welch, P. J. Scott, William Frosch.

FRANK H. MESSER,

(Successor to CHARLES S. PARKER,)

Funeral Director and Embalmer,

—AND DEALER IN—

Caskets, Black Walnut & Whitewood Coffins,

METALLIC CASKETS.

Cloth-Covered Caskets a Specialty.

THIBET, LAWN AND CAMBRIC ROBES.

Every kind of Funeral Furnishings made at short notice.

HACKS, CARRIAGES AND FLOWERS

FURNISHED IF DESIRED.

Residence, Elm Street, near Elm Square.

Warerooms, PARK STREET, ANDOVER.

✻ ELM HOUSE ✻

C. F. GRUBER, PROPRIETOR.

Pleasantly Situated near Depot and Business Center.

BOARD BY THE DAY OR WEEK.

Parties Accommodated at Short Notice.

Good Livery and Boarding Stable.

ELM SQUARE, ANDOVER, MASS.

ESSEX COUNTY.

COUNTY OFFICERS.

JUDGE OF PROBATE AND INSOLVENCY.—Rollin E. Harmon, Lynn.

REGISTER OF PROBATE AND INSOLVENCY.—Jeremiah T. Mahony, Salem.

SHERIFF.—Samuel A. Johnson, Lawrence.

CLERK OF COURTS.—Dean Peabody, Lynn.

COUNTY TRAESURER.—E. Kendall Jenkins, Andover.

REGISTERS OF DEEDS.—Northern District: John J. Donovan, Lawrence; Southern District: Charles S. Osgood, Salem.

COUNTY COMMISSIONERS.—Horace F. Longfellow, Newbury; Edward B. Bishop, Haverhill; John M. Danforth, Lynnfield.

SPECIAL COMMISSIONERS.—Nelson P. Cummings, Amesbury; Thomas F. Pedrick. Lynnfield.

COMMISSIONERS OF INSOLVENCY.—Benjamin C. Ames, Lawrence; Harry J. Cole, Haverhill; William D. Chapple, Salem.

MASTERS OF CHANCERY.—Newton P. Frye, North Andover; Nathaniel C. Bartlett, Haverhill; Henri N. Woods, Rockport; Charles W. Richardson, Salem; Nathan D. A. Clarke, Swampscott; Nathaniel J. Holden, Salem.

TRIAL JUSTICES.—J. Scott Todd, Rowley; William M. Rogers, Methuen; Orlando B. Tenney, Georgetown; George H. Poor, Andover; Amos Merrill, Peabody; William Nutting, Jr., Marblehead; Charles A. Sayward, Ipswich; Stephen Gilman, Lynnfield; Joseph T. Wilson, Nahant; William C. Fabens, Marblehead; George L. Weil, North Andover; George M. Amerige, Saugus.

PATRICK BURKE,

—DEALER IN—

DRY AND FANCY GOODS,

—ALSO,—

A Full Line of Boys' and Youths'

CLOTHING.

Village Street, Andover, Mass.

MISS ANNIE E. BURKE,

FASHIONABLE DRESSMAKER.

Ladies' and Children's Suits

Cut and made with careful attention to wants of customers.

VILLAGE STREET, ANDOVER, MASS.

T. J. FARMER,

—DEALER IN—

FISH, : OYSTERS,

Lobsters, Clams,

And CANNED GOODS.

Fresh, Salt, Smoked and Pickled Fish.

ALL KINDS OF

FRESH FISH

IN THEIR SEASON.

All orders promptly delivered.

Post-Office Avenue.

POST-OFFICES.

ANDOVER POST-OFFICE.

William G. Goldsmith, Postmaster; George T. Abbott, Assistant Postmaster; J. Percy Roberts, Clerk. Office hours, 7 a. m. to 8 p. m.

MONEY ORDER OFFICE.—Office hours, 8 a. m. to 6 p. m.; holidays, 8 to 9.30 a. m. and 5 to 6 p. m.

MAIL ARRANGEMENTS.

Mails close: For Boston, New York, South and West, 7 a. m.; Lawrence, North and East, *8 a. m.; Boston, New York, South and West, 10 a. m.; Boston, New York, South and West, *11.50 a. m.; Lawrence, 11.50 a. m.; Lawrence, North and East, *3.40 p. m.; Lawrence, Boston, New York, South and West, *6.30 p. m.

Railroad post-office mails.

Mails ready for delivery: From Boston, New York, South and West, 8 a. m.; Boston (way stations) and Lawrence, 9 a. m.; Lawrence, North and East, 1.30 p. m; Boston, 4.30 p. m.; Boston, New York, South and West, 5 p. m.; Lawrence and North, 6.30 p. m.; Boston, New York, South and West, 7.15 p. m.; Lawrence and East, 7.30 p. m.

BALLARD VALE POST-OFFICE.

C. H. Marland, Postmaster.

Mails arrive from Boston, East and North, 8.18 a. m., 12.30, 12.45, 4 35, 5.50 and 7.15 p. m.; mails close, 7.30 and 11 a. m.; 5.30 p. m.

POSTAGE RATES.

DOMESTIC MAIL MATTER.

FIRST CLASS.—Letters, two cents per ounce or fraction thereof. Sealed packages, two cents per ounce or fraction thereof.

SECOND CLASS.—Papers sent by publishers, or from office of publication, one cent per pound.

Papers of the second class, when sent by other than publishers, four ounces one cent.

THIRD CLASS.—Books, circulars, photographs, lithographs, proof sheets, and corrected proof sheets with manuscript copy accompanying the same, one cent for two ounces.

FOURTH CLASS.—Labels, billheads, wrapping paper, merchandise, to the extent of four pounds, one cent per ounce, except seeds, cuttings, roots and plants, one cent for two ounces or fraction thereof.

Letters with a special delivery stamp thereon, in addition to the regular postage, are delivered by special messenger from any post-office in the United States.

From the Andover office money can be sent to any office doing money-order business in the United States or foreign countries. From the Ballard Vale office money can be sent to any office doing money-order business in the United States.

A single domestic money order may include any amount from one cent to one hundred dollars, inclusive, but must not contain a fractional part of a cent.

Postal notes for any sum not exceeding $4.99 are issued at a charge of three cents each.

FOREIGN MAIL MATTER.

For countries of the Universal Postal Union: Letters, five cents for one-half ounce or fraction thereof. Books, papers, photographs, one cent for each two ounces or fraction thereof. Merchandise not transmissible except at letter rates.

JAMES DORMAN,
Mason, Contractor & Builder.

PLANS, SPECIFICATIONS and ESTIMATES

FURNISHED FOR

Buildings of Brick or Stone, of any Style of Architecture.

HAND & STEAM DERRICKS & ENGINES

TO LET.

Residence, 116 Cross Street, Lawrence, Mass.

EDUCATIONAL.

ANDOVER THEOLOGICAL SEMINARY.

Chartered June 19, 1807.

BOARD OF TRUSTEES.—President, Rev. Daniel T. Fiske, D. D., Newburyport; Clerk, Rev. Cecil F. P. Bancroft, Ph. D., LL. D., Andover; Treasurer, Alpheus Hardy, B. A., Boston; Rev. Joshua W. Wellman, D. D., Malden; Thomas H. Russell, M. A., Boston; Hon. Joseph S. Ropes, M. A., Boston; Rev. Alexander McKenzie, D. D., LL. D., Cambridge; Rev. William H. Wilcox, D. D., LL. D., Malden; Hon. Robert R. Bishop, M. A., Newton Center; President Franklin Carter, Ph. D., LL. D., Williamstown; Rev. James G. Vose, D. D., Providence, R. I.; Hon. Rowland Hazzard, M. A., Peacedale, R. I.; Thomas M. Osborn, Esq., Salem.

FACULTY.—Rev. Edwards A. Park, Rev. John P. Gulliver, Rev. Egbert G. Smyth, Rev. John Phelps Taylor, Rev. J. Wesley Churchill, Rev. George Harris, Rev. Edward Y. Hincks, Rev. William H. Ryder, Rev. George F. Moore, Rev. Theodore C. Pease. Rev. William L. Ropes, Librarian.

ABBOT ACADEMY.

TRUSTEES.—Prof. Edwards A. Park, D. D., LL. D., President; Warren F. Draper, Esq., Treasurer; Col. George Ripley, Clerk; Hon. Rufus S. Frost, Rev. Edward G. Porter, Prof. John Wesley Churchill, Mortimer B. Mason, Esq., Horace H. Tyer, Esq., Prof. John Phelps Taylor, Mrs. John M. Harlow, Mrs. Willard G. Sperry.

TEACHERS.—Laura S. Watson, A. M., Principal; Maria Stockbridge Merrill, Elizabeth M. Chadbourne, Jane Lincoln Greeley, Katherine R. Kelsey, Natalie Shiefferdecker, Alice Julia Hamlin, Edith Elizabeth Ingalls, Nellie M. Mason, Katherine I. Hutchinson, A. M., Lilian Northrop Stoddard, A. B., Prof. Samuel Morse Downs, Jennie B. Ladd, Clara L. Carlton, Angelica S. Patterson, Prof. Henri Morand.

MATRONS.—Miss Angelica Kimball, at Draper Hall; Miss Mary E. Kelley, at Smith Hall.

PHILLIPS ACADEMY.

Organized in 1778.

TRUSTEES.—Same as for Andover Theological Seminary.

FACULTY.—Cecil F. P. Bancroft, Ph. D., LL. D., Principal, on the Peter Smith Byers Memorial Foundation; Matthew S. McCurdy, M. A., instructor in Mathematics; William B. Graves, M. A., Professor of Natural Sciences, on the George Peabody Foundation; George T. Eaton, M. A., Instructor in Mathematics; George D. Pettee, B. A., Instructor in Mathematics, and Registrar; William H. Terrill, M. A., Instructor in Greek and Latin; Charles E. Stone, Ph. B., Instructor in French; Charles H. Forbes, B. A., Instructor in Latin, on the John C. Phillips Foundation; Henry W. Boynton, B. A., Instructor in English; Bernard M. Allen, B. A., Instructor in Latin and English Studies; Walter R. Newton, B. A., Instructor in German; Clifford H. Moore, B. A., Professor of Greek; Archibald A. Freeman, M. A., Instructor in History; Allen R. Benner, B. A., Instructor in Latin and English studies, George W. Benedict, B. A., Instructor in Latin and English studies; James C. Graham, B. S., Instructor in Natural Sciences; . Prof. John Wesley Churchill, M. A., Instructor in Elocution.

PUBLIC SCHOOLS.

SCHOOL BOARD, 1893.

Prof. F. O. Baldwin, John Alden, C. H. Shattuck, J. Newton Cole, John Nelson Cole, William Odlin, Mrs. L. A. Wilson. W. A. Baldwin, Secretary and Superintendent. Office hours from 4 to 5 p. m. Truant Officers: Center, Barnett Rogers; West Parish, Michael Welch; Ballard Vale, Joseph Scott.

TEACHERS.

CENTRAL GRAMMAR SCHOOL.—Susan M. Wilbur, Principal; Jessie B. F. Greene, Dollie M. Farnum, Frances W. Meldrum, Anna E. Chase.

SOUTH CENTER SCHOOL.—Sara Smith, Principal; Sarah McNulty, Annie O. Clemons, Lucy A. Roach, Jennie S. Abbott, Laura F. Farnum.

BALLARD VALE SCHOOL.—Susan W. Molther, Principal; Caroline A. Deane, Mary F. Brown, Rubina S. Copeland, Florence Abbott, Ida G. Goldthwaite.

ABBOT VILLAGE SCHOOL.—Margaret C. Donovan, Principal; Jennie Birnie, Maria D. McLoud.

FRYE VILLAGE SCHOOL.—Agnes C. Morrison, Principal; Lilla Abbott, Helen W. Battles.

WEST CENTER SCHOOL.—Hannah R. Bailey, Principal; Mary B. Hardy.
SCOTLAND SCHOOL.—Carrie B. Deane.
HOLT SCHOOL.—Harriet W. Ryder.
OSGOOD SCHOOL.—Lilla B. Robinson.
BAILEY SCHOOL.—Eva A. Hardy.
NORTH SCHOOL.—Ida J. Holt.
TEACHER OF DRAWING.—Emilie B. Stefan.
MUSIC.—Edward Butterworth.
PUNCHARD FREE SCHOOL.—Trustees: Rev. J. J. Blair, Samuel H. Boutwell, Cnarles H. Gilbert, George Guild, Rev. W. F. Greene, Rev. Frederick Palmer, George H. Poor, Horace H. Tyer. Teachers: Frank O. Baldwin, Principal; Mary E. Dern, Mary A. Abbott, Lucia G. Merrill.

Population, 1890 census,	6142
Number of children in town over five and under fifteen,	1011
Number of children of all ages registered in primary, intermediate and grammar schools,	1063
Average registration,	910.4
Average attendance,	809.20
Average per cent of attendance,	88.8

CHARLES O. CUMMINGS,

Elm Street, - corner Washington Avenue.

REAL ESTATE.

DESIRABLE HOUSE LOTS for sale on WASHINGTON AVENUE

On terms to suit the purchaser.

Send for prices, etc.   P. O. BOX 402.

CHARLES M. MUSTER,

(Successor to C. A. BOONE,)

CARRIAGE
— AND —
SIGN PAINTER

All work guaranteed.

Shop, corner Park and Bartlett Streets, Andover.

WILLIAM F. TRULAND,

VARIETY STORE,

Essex Street, below Boston & Maine Railroad,

ANDOVER.

WILLIAM POOR,

— MANUFACTURER OF —

EXPRESS, GROCERY, MILK AND ORDER

WAGONS,

Farm Carts, &c.

Our Specialty, Meat and Market Wagons.

CARRIAGE PAINTING AND REPAIRING.

BLACKSMITH WORK OF ALL KINDS.

All work warranted as represented. Call and get our prices.

MAIN STREET,   FRYE VILLAGE.

FIRE DEPARTMENT.

BOARD OF ENGINEERS.—Lewis T. Hardy, Chief; George D. Lawson, Clerk; N. E. Mears, Andrew McTernen.

ANDOVER STEAMER, No. 1.

Park street. Foreman, Frank Hodges; First Assistant, George Holt; Second Assistant, S. M. Goodwin; Clerk, George A. Morse; Engineer, J. S. Harnden; First Driver, F. M. Smith; Second Driver, J. Napier; Third Driver, O. Carter; 21 call men.

HOSE CARRIAGE, No. 1.

First Assistant in charge.

B. FRANK SMITH HOOK AND LADDER TRUCK.

Second Assistant in charge.

J. P. BRADLEE STEAMER, No. 2.

Ballard Vale. Foreman, E. H. Shattuck; Assistant Foreman, J. J. Haggerty; Clerk, Carl Hoffman; Treasurer, John Riley; Steward, J. H. Clinton; 16 call men.

SMITH & MANNING,

—DEALERS IN—

Dry and Fancy Goods,

GROCERIES, FLOUR, GRAIN, ETC.

Crockery, ✻ Glassware,

CARPETINGS AND PAPER-HANGINGS.

ESSEX STREET, ANDOVER.

J. L. SMITH. A. S. MANNING.

T. A. HOLT & CO.,

—DEALERS IN—

Dry Goods and Groceries,

CENTRAL STREET, corner Essex,

ANDOVER, MASS.

Branch store at North Andover.

Andover Resident Directory.

ABBREVIATIONS USED.

Av., avenue; A. D., Abbot District; A. V., Abbot Village; bds., boards; B., Boston; B. D., Bailey District; B. V., Ballard Vale; c., corner; ct., court; C. & K., Craighead & Kentz; emp., employe; h., house; F. D., Frye District; F. V., Frye Village; H. D., Holt District; M. V., Marland Village; n., near; N. D., North District; O. D., Osgood District; opp., opposite; P. D., Phillips District; pl., place; r., rear; sq., square; S. D., Scotland District; C. D., Central District; W. C., West Center District; W. P., West Parish.

A

ABBOTT ABBIE H. MRS. (Albert) house Main near Porter
" Allen F. carpenter, boards Mrs. Sarah E. Upton
" Almon P. painter, house North District
" Anna B. Miss, house Mrs. Elizabeth L. do.
" Andrew J. tin peddler, house High
" Betsey Mrs. (J. Thompson) house Essex

ABBOTT CHARLES E., M. D. physician and surgeon, office and residence 43 Main. Office hours, 8 to 9 a. m., 1 to 3 and 6 to 8 p. m.

" Charlotte H. Miss, house Draper block, Main
" Charles M. Mrs. house 22 Essex
" Charlotte S. Miss, house Punchard av. near Main
" Edward F. emp. B. & M. car shop, house near the church, W. P.
" Elizabeth L. Mrs. (Nathan B.) house East Chestnut
" Ellen J. Miss, house Mrs. H. E. Giddings
" Ezra Lincoln, bookkeeper, house 55 Central

Abbott Freeman R. butcher, house Essex cor. Baker's lane
" George T. asst. postmaster, house Elm cor. Summer
" Hannah Mrs. (Moody) house Lowell, F. V.
" Hannah Miss, house Hartwell B. do.
" Hannah B. Miss, dressmaker, h. Bartlett cor. Chestnut
" Harry P. teaming, house Lowell, W. P.
" Hartwell B. farmer, house Mineral near railroad bridge
" James A. carpenter, house Punchard av. near Chestnut
" James J. farmer, house Mineral near railroad bridge
" John B. farmer, house Main, S. D.
" John L. farmer, house 40 Central
" John W. emp. Tyer Rubber Co. house William W. do.
" Joseph, house High near Elm square
" Joseph T. tinsmith E. Pike, house Maple av. near Elm
" Lilla Miss, teacher piano-forte, house Mrs. Abbie H. do.
" Mary A. Miss, teacher, house Hartwell B. do.
" Mary E. Miss, house Essex
" Mary J. Mrs. (Charles) house Main, S. D.
" Mary S. Miss, house Mrs. Rhoda do.
" Nathan F. farmer, house off Summer n. Washington av.
" Rhoda Mrs. (Sylvester) house Porter, P. D.
" Sarah F. Mrs. (Sereno T.) house Main cor. Morton
" Nathan G. farmer, house near Lawrence line, N. D.
" Stephen E. farmer, house Chestnut Hill farm, S. D.
" Timothy, farmer, house Mineral near railroad bridge
" Tryphena M. Mrs. (Moses) house South Main
" Warren G. farmer, h. from river road to West Parish
" William, house 47 Central
" William H. emp. Tyer Rubber Co. house North Main near railroad bridge
" William W. emp. Tyer Rubber Co. h. off Lowell, F. V.
Abercrombie Eliza Miss, house 16 Brick block, A. V.
" Emma Miss, weaver, house George Simpson
" James, emp. Smith & Dove, house near village, A. V.
Adams Charles A. house Center District
" Charles F. farm hand, house William H. Tucker
" John J. emp. Tyer Rubber Co. house Post Office av.
" Lydia E. Mrs. (Alfred) house Salem, H. D.
Alden John, chemist Pacific mills, Lawrence, h. Punchard av. n. Main
" William, supt. of schools, h. Washington av. near Elm
Allen Hannah L. Mrs. (George W.) house Webster Hazelwood
" Martha M. Mrs. house Henry S. Robinson
Allican Herbert A. laborer, house John J. Murphy
" J. Henry, emp. J. W. Barnard, house North Main near Tyer Rubber Co.
" Philip, laborer, house Morton

Allican Samuel, house Center District
" Simon, laborer, boards Timothy O'Connell
Amiro Antoine, carpenter, boards John Stack, Jr.
Anderson David, flax dresser, house 5 Brick block, A. V.
" Isabella Mrs. (Samuel) house Cuba
" James, house Ballard Vale
" James B. emp. Smith & Dove, house Cuba
ANDERSON JOHN S. (Anderson & Bowman) house Cuba
" Peter, house Haverhill, F. V.
Andrews Eugene, carpenter, house Punchard av. near Park
" Frederick A. clerk, house 52 Main
" James, emp. Stevens mill, boards Mrs. Mary Lord
" Lucien J. carpenter, boards George Cummings
" Menzies C. house 52 Main
Angus William, emp. Smith & Dove, house Mineral
Ashness Harry, spinner, house Harding near railroad bridge
" William, foreman spinning room. Stevens mill, house North Main cor. Marland
Ashton Orrell, janitor B. V. school house, house River, B. V.
Ashworth James, shoemaker, house Andover, B. V.
Atchison William, house North Main
Austin Maggie, domestic, house Mrs. Charles B. Gould
Auty William A. wool sorter, house Joshua Hirst

B

BABINE JOSEPH, house Frye Village
" John M. house Frye Village
" Nelson, house Frye Village
Bacigalupo Louis J. (L. J. Bacigalupo & Co.) fruit, Main, house East Chestnut
Bailey Albert, farmer, house off river road, W. P.
" Charles L. house Osgood District
" David M. emp. Smith & Dove, house Brick block, A. V.
" Edward W. house Bailey District
" Frank E. house Bailey District
" George W. carpenter, house Poor, F. V.
" Henry H. house Abbot District
" John B. house Bailey District
" Joshua, farmer, house Poor, F. V.
" Moses A. house Abbot District
" Nathan R. house North District
" Palmer, farmer, house off river road, W. P.
" Rufus, house North District
" Samuel G. farmer, house river road, W. P.

Bailey S. Gilman, prop. Shadyside grove, house Lowell near Haggett's pond, W. P.
" Samuel H. farmer, house Porter, P. D.
" Timothy P. house Abbot District
" Warren A. house Abbot District
Baker Alexander, emp. J. P. Butterfield, house do.
" Arthur W. farmer, house Salem, H. D.
" Charles, iceman, house off Main, S. D.
" George F. farmer, house off Mineral near railroad bridge, W. P.
" Howard, house Phillips District
" John H. farm hand, house Salem, H. D.
" Wellesley, house Holt District
Balch George H. farmer, house Central near Main
Baldwin Charles B. clerk C. P. R. R. house Curtis M. do.
" Clara J. bookkeeper Emerson Mfg. Co. h. Curtis M. do.
" Curtis M. janitor of Punchard high school building, house Summer near Punchard av.
" F. O. principal high school, house Bartlett near Punchard av.
" John F. house High near Elm square
Ballard Mary A. Miss, house Main c. Punchard av.
Bancroft Albert, farmer, house off Main, S. D.
" Albert M. stone mason, house off Main, S. D.
" Cecil F. P. Dr. principal of Phillips Academy, house Chapel av.
" Cecil K. student, house Dr. Cecil F. P. do.
Bannister Wilson Mrs. house off Lowell, B. V.
Barker Maria A. Mrs. (Amos R.) h. Mrs. Sarah A. M. Loring
Barnard Charles B. house Edwin H. do.
" Edwin H. painter and paper hanger, Essex, h. Central
" H. Gertrude Miss, house Jacob W. do.
" Henry W. shoe mfr. Barnard ct. house Jacob W. do.
" Horatio, farmer, house Lowell, W. P.
" Jacob W. shoe mfr. house Main c. High
" Lydia H. Miss, millinery, house Centre, B. V.
" Susan O. Mrs. (Jacob) house Post Office av.
Barnet Charlotte Mrs. (William) house High
" Catherine, house Mrs. Charlotte do.
Barrett Kate, domestic, house T. Dennie Thomson
" John, farmer, house Haverhill n. railroad bridge, F. V.
" Patrick, emp. Stevens mill, house Marland, M. V.
" William, emp. Smith & Dove, house Haverhill, F. V.
Barry Frances, house Mrs. Mary do.
" Mary Mrs. (John) house Morton
Battles Otis W. emp. Smith & Dove, house Lowell
Baxter Jessie Mrs. house David Anderson

Bean Jonathan M. hairdresser, P. O. block, house Maple av. near Walnut av.
Beard F. R. Mrs. (Harris P.) house Lowell, W. P.
Beeley Henry A. machinist, house Andover, B. V.
Belknap Lyman A. house Central
Bell Charles H. house Poor, F. V.
" Charles H. Jr. emp. Hathaway, Soule & Harrington, B. house Charles H. do.
" Clara M. house Charles H. do.
" John W. asst. treas. Smith & Dove, h. Haverhill, F. V.
" Robert, janitor town hall, house Maple av.
Bennie Flora Mrs. house Sand, B. V.
Benson Olof, emp. George W. W. Dove, house Main near the bridge, F. V.
Bentley Thomas H. painter, house Haverhill near the railroad bridge, F. V.
Berry Fred P. clerk Maverick Oil Co. house East Chestnut c. Punchard av.
" Dora S. Miss, house 15 Salem

BERRY J. WARREN, (T. A. Holt & Co.) house Chestnut c. Punchard av.

Billington Charles F. wool sorter, house Andover, B. V.
Binbine John M. carpenter, house Haverhill c. Main, F. V.
Bird Daniel, house Osgood District
" Lawrence, farm hand, house Boston road, B. V.
Birnie David, emp. Smith & Dove, house Main, F. V.
" Jennie, teacher, house David do.
" John W. house David do.
" Otis W. emp. Smith & Dove, house David do.
Black Hugh, house Charles E. Donovan
Blackburn Nellie E. Mrs. (Franklin B.) boards Benjamin Brown
Blair Isabel Mrs. house John S. Harris
Blake Emily Mrs. (Peter) house Main, F. V.
" Hannah L. Mrs. (Rev. Joseph) house 10 Abbot
" Harriet Miss, house Mrs. Hannah L. do.
" William, farmer, h. off Lowell n. J. W. Mooar's, W. P.
" Sarah, house Mrs. Emily do.
" Susan M. Miss, teacher, house Mrs. Hannah L. do.
Blamire James, emp. Smith & Dove, house Main, F. V.
Blanchard Amos, treas. B. & M. R. R. house Phillips n. Abbot
Blois Charles S. expressman, rooms Post Office av.
Blood George W. house West Center District
Bliss Arthur, druggist, Main, house High
Blunt Charles C. farmer, house 51 Salem, P. D.
" Joseph H. farmer, house Charles C. do.
" Lucy J. Mrs. (Samuel W.) house 88 Main
Bodge Wilbert M. emp. Rev. E. C. Smyth, h. off Salem, H. D.

Bodwell Charles A. house Mrs. Emma A. do.
" Emma A. Mrs. (Henry A.) house Maple av.
" E. Grace, house Mrs. Emma A. do.
" Fred A. painter, house F. Lewis do.
" F. Lewis, painter, house Park
" Myra J. dressmaker, house Mrs. Emma A. do.
Bond Mortimer, house Abbot District
Bonner Edward, emp. Bradlee mill, house River, B. V.
" James J. emp. C. & K. house Edward do.
" William G. emp. Bradlee mill, house Edward do.
Booth Charles A. house Punchard av. near Main
" James, hostler, boards Elm House
Bossoneau Azarde, emp. C. & K. h. Blaney block, Andover, B. V.
Bourdelais Henry, carpenter, house Lowell, O. D.
" Joseph, farmer, house Lowell, O. D.
Boutwell Arthur T. house Bailey District
" Chester N. house Bailey District
" Edward W. market gardener, house Bailey District
" Frederick S. clerk Andover Savings Bank, boards Mrs. Elizabeth L. Abbott
" George, farmer, h. West Andover road to Lowell, B. D.
" Lewis B. T. house Bailey District
" Samuel H. farmer, house Bailey District
" Walter B. house Bailey District

BOWMAN CHARLES, (J. S. Anderson & Charles Bowman) horseshoers, Park, house Bartlett
" Charles Mrs. house Village opp. Cuba
" William, tinsmith, house Village opp. Cuba
Boyle Elizabeth A. house Maple av. near Elm
" James, emp. Stevens mill, house Marland, M. V.
" Rose, house James Boyle
Boynton Benjamin, market gardener, house Lowell near the church, W. P.
" Clara R. teacher piano and organ, house Benjamin do.
" Henry, farmer, house Lowell, O. D.
Brackett Walter N. house Center District
Bradley Joseph M. tailor, Main, house Walnut av.
Bradshaw James O. boxmaker, house Brook
" Richard, emp. Smith & Dove, house Brook
Bradstreet G. Allen, ice cream maker, boards Central Street Dining Room
Brennan Mary F. boards Charles E. Torrey
" Patrick H. emp. Stevens mill, boards Charles E. Torrey
Breslin Mary Mrs. house Marland, M. V.
Brown Alexander, foreman Smith & Dove, house Lowell, F. V.
" Benjamin, boots, shoes and rubbers, house Park near Punchard av.

Brown David, moulder, house Centre, B. V.
" Fanny Miss, house Morton near Main
" Edwin, switchman, Lowell Junction, h. Marland, B. V.
" Frank A. conductor electric railway, house Bartlett
" George A. clerk Benjamin Brown, house Park near Punchard av.
" Julia M. Miss, house Andover, B. V.
" James A. house Phillips District
" Lemuel, coachman, house Pearson
" Mary Miss, house Morton near Main
" Mary F. Miss, teacher, house Andover, B. V.
" Michael, moulder, house Tewksbury, B. V.
" Nancy B. Mrs. (Brown & Shattuck) millinery, dry goods, etc., Carter's block, Main, house Bartlett
" Waldo, farmer, house off Salem, Jenkins' Corner, H. D.
" William G. meat and provisions, High, house High near Harding
Brownell Henry, laborer, house off Salem, H. D.
" Charles H. carpenter, house Lowell, W. P.
Bruce David F. flaxdresser, house Village near Cuba
" Ralph, teamster, Bradlee mills, house Sand, B. V.
Brundrett Fred W. house North District
" James H. house North District
Buchan Charles S. upholsterer, boards Frank A. Dinsmore
" George, emp. Smith & Dove, house off Lowell near J. W. Mooar's, W. P.
" George W. watchman Smith & Dove, house George do.
" John S. plumber, house George do.
Buck Alice Miss, house Walter do.
" Cassius W. painter, house Center District
" Louis G. commercial salesman, house Silas do.
" Silas, teaming and jobbing, house Marland, B. V.
" Walter, real estate, house School c. Morton
Buckley Joanna, domestic, house Amos Blanchard
" Catherine Miss, house Ridge
" Daniel J. emp. A. W. W. house School c. Ridge
" Jeremiah, farm hand, house John B. Withum
" John J. stone mason, h. North Main n. railroad bridge
" William, house Marland, B. V.

BURKE ANNIE E. dressmaker, house Patrick do.

" Edward J. carriage painter, house Patrick do.
" John, spinner, house Andover, B. V.
" Nellie, emp. Bradlee mill, house John do.

BURKE PATRICK, dry and fancy goods, house Village, A. V.

" William E. emp. Bradlee mill, house John do.

Burnett Howard, house Osgood District
Burnham George, supt. Andover almshouse, house do.
" George H. farmer, h. off Lowell at J. W. Mooar's, W. P.
" George H. Jr. men's furnishings, Lawrence, house George H. do.
Burns John, section hand B. & M. R. R. house Andover, B. V.
" John, Jr. brass polisher, house John do.
" John H. coachman, house Mrs. Nancy do.
" Nancy Mrs. (David) house Summer opp. Washington av.
" William, tailor, house Mrs. Nancy do.
Burrill Lucy Miss, boards Miss Mary W. Towne
Bursley George L. house Phillips District
Burtt Albert B. emp. Hardy & Cole, h. North Main n. Marland
" Angie M. house William A. do.
" Edward W. market gardener, house Lowell, W. P.
" Hannah E. Mrs. (Henry) house Elm
" M. Winnie, house Mrs. Hannah E. do.
" William A. farmer, house Lowell, W. P.
" William E. receiving clerk B. & M. R. R. house Bartlett near Morton
" William H. farmer, house Lowell, W. P.
Butterfield Belle J. elocutionist, house James P. do.
" James P. house School near Morton
Butterworth John, emp. Stevens mill, boards James E. Qualey
Buxton George H. farmer, house Mrs. Lucy do.
" Ira, emp. Cole & Hardy, bds. Mrs. Margaret Doherty
" Lewis, farm hand, boards Plato Eames
" Lucy Mrs. (Elijah) house Main n. North Reading line
Byers Alfred S. (Sagehomme & Byers) house Railroad near B. & M. R. R. station
" Charlotte Mrs. (James) h. Railroad n. B. & M. station
" Esther Mrs. (John) house Central
Byrnes Bridget, domestic, house Rev. Edwards A. Park

C

CAFFERY ELLEN MISS, house Philip do.
" James, emp. Bradlee mill, house River, B. V.
" John, emp. Bradlee mill, house Oak, B. V.
" Mary A. Mrs. house Nathan H. Shattuck
" Owen F. emp. Bradlee mill, house James do.
" Philip, laborer, house Tewksbury, B. V.
" Thomas E. emp. Bradlee mill, house John do.
" William, emp. Bradlee mill, house Tewksbury, B. V.
" William, Jr. house William do.
Cahill William, house Bailey District

Caldwell Albert W. painter, High, house Florence
" George R. carpenter, house 6 Washington av.
" William U. house Summer c. Washington av.
Callahan Annie, domestic, house Mrs. Ella T. Cheever
" James, emp. Stevens mill, house Marland, M. V.
" Johanna, domestic, house Miss Ella T. Cheever
" Mary A. Mrs. (Robert) house Abbot
" William E. house Ballard Vale
Callum James A. house Abbot Village
" John B. emp. Smith & Dove, house Village, A. V.
Cameron James, emp. Tyer Rubber Co. house Mrs. Margaret do.
" Margaret Mrs. house Village near the bridge, A. V.
Campbell James, engineer Smith & Dove, house Haverhill, F. V.
Campion John H. grocer, Elm square, rooms Edward Trefry
Canfield Horace J. house 26 School
" J. H. Mrs. house 26 School
Capstic Sarah J. Miss, domestic, h. Mrs. Grace M. Whittemore
Carey Catherine Mrs. house Andover, B. V.
" Dennis J. emp. Stevens mill, h. North Main n. Harding
CARLTON FRANK T. correspondent Tyer Rubber Co. house 50 Central
Carney Daniel, laborer, boards John J. Buckley
Carpenter C. C. Rev. house Bartlett near Morton
" Harry, house Osgood District
" John T. house Village District
Carrie James B. emp. Smith & Dove, house Poor, F. V.
Carruth Clarissa Mrs. (Sumner) house Isaac do.
" Helen E. Mrs. (Isaac S.) house East Chestnut
" Isaac, farmer, house Lowell, O. D.
Carter Charles L. house off East Chestnut, Carter's hill
" Emily, house 92 Main
" George N. house North District
" James Mrs. dressmaker, house James O. do.
" James O. emp. J. T. Lovejoy, house Pearson
" Justin, Jr. farmer, house Mrs. Rebecca do.
" W. Otis, emp. H. P. Noyes, house James O. do.
" Rebecca A. Mrs. house off Main, S. D.
" Susan R. teacher, house Mrs. Rebecca do.
" Ulysses G. house North District
" William H. carpenter, house off Main, S. D.
Casey Patrick, house Bailey District
Cates Abraham L. emp. B. F. Smith, house Central n. Phillips
Cavanaugh Michael, wool scourer, house Patrick J. Scott
Chadwick Susan B. Mrs. (George) house Chestnut
Chandler Emily, house Elm near Walnut av.
" Frances E. house Elm near Walnut av.

CHANDLER GEORGE W. coal, wood, etc., Main, h. High
" John, house East Chestnut
" John H. books, stationery, etc. Main, house Maple av.
" Joshua H. farmer, h. off Lowell at J. W. Mooar's, W. P.
" Laura M. dressmaker, house Elm near Walnut av.
CHANDLER MARION R. teacher piano-forte, h. George W. do.
" Phebe A. Mrs. (Heman P.) h. Mrs. Mary A. Ballard
Chapin Edward P. supt. Washington mills, Lawrence, house Phillips near Abbot
Chapman Eliza Mrs. (Richard) house Lowell c. Main, F. V.
" Ovid, variety store and dining room, Main near Morton, house do.
Charnley William, house Elm near the square
CHASE HERBERT F. machinist and agent Columbia bicycles, Post Office av. house Elm
" Miriam Mrs. (Albee) house Elm near Walnut av.
CHASE OMAR P. pres. and manager Andover orchestra, house Elm c. Washington av.
" Wallace N. shoemaker, h. Blaney block, Andover, B. V.
Cheever Benjamin, shoemaker, house off Main, S. D.
" Charles, farmer, house off Main, S. D.
" Ella T. house Main junc. School
" George F. chief of police, house Maple av. n. Walnut av.
" Samuel O. farmer, house off Main, S. D.
" Sarah S. house Main junc. School
" William B. clerk T. A. Holt & Co. house Bartlet c. Chestnut
Chickering Milton, carpenter, house Essex
" Otis, teacher, house 22 Essex
" Samuel, commercial salesman, house 22 Essex
Christie George A. emp. J. N. Cole, bds. Mrs. Sarah E. Upton
" Robert, emp. Tyer Rubber Co. boards Barnett Rogers
Church Arabella W. Mrs. (Frederick L.) house 50 Central
" Hannibal H. house 77 Main near the bridge, F. V.
" Helen M. copyist, State House, B. h. Hannibal H. do.
Churchill Donald, house Main c. Phillips
" John W. Rev. prof. Theological Seminary, house Main c. Phillips
Claflin John M. emp. Bradlee mill, house Marland c. Tewksbury, B. V.
Clark Alfred D. farmer, house off Salem, H. D.
" A. Thompson, house Ballard Vale
" Charles A. engineer Tyer Rubber Co. house North Main near Pearson

Clark Charles W. shipper W. H. Raymond, B. house Summer near Punchard av.
" Dorcas A. Mrs. house Timothy Abbott
" Edith, house Jesse H. do.
" Jesse H. farmer, house Highland road c. Salem
" Joseph W. foreman Hardy & Cole, h. High c. Harding
" Justin E. telegraph operator, house Mineral junc. Cuba
" Lewis, engineer, house Centre, B. V.
" Lucia F. teacher Wellesley college, h. Mrs. Susan M. do.
" Sarah M. Mrs. house James A. Eaton
" Susan M. Mrs. (Almon) house Summer n. Punchard av.
" William J. farmer, house Lowell, W. P.
" William M. teamster, house Main, F. V.
Clement Millard A. clerk T. A. Holt & Co. house 34 Park
Clemons Albert E. switchman B. & M. R. R. h. Marland, B. V.
" Annie O. S. teacher, house Albert E. do.
" Katherine M. milliner, house Albert E. do.
" Maynard E. house Albert E. do.
" William S. baggage master, house Marland, B. V.
" Robert R. house Ballard Vale
Clinton John H. cigars, tobacco, etc. house Clinton court off Andover, B. V.
" Sarah Mrs. (Thomas H.) house Clinton court off Andover, B. V.
" Thomas, Jr. house Ballard Vale
Closs Jane Mrs. house Essex near the railroad
Clough Elizabeth, house Salem near Chapel av.
" George W. house Centre
Clukey Henry L. carpenter, house Centre, B. V.
Coates James, house River, B. V.
" James, Jr. emp. C. & K. house James do.
" John, emp. C. & K. house River, B. V.
" Oliver T. emp. Bradlee mill, house James do.
Coburn Helen G. Mrs. (George W.) house Central near School
Cochran George H. farmer, house Lowell, F. V.
" James H. farmer, house Punchard av. near Main
" John W. house James H. do.
" Parker E. printer, house James H. do.
Coffin George H. clerk, house Lowell, B. V.
Cogswell Lucy, house Henry E. Gould
Colange Ann Mrs. house Essex c. Railroad
Colby J. S. house Salem near Highland road, P. D.
Cole George S. deputy sheriff, house Chestnut
COLE JOHN N. manager Andover Press and prop. Andover Book Store, house Locke
" J. Newton, emp. Frederick Ames, B. house East Chestnut near Main

Cole John T. emp. Tyer Rubber Co. house Mineral n. the bridge
" Joseph F. (Hardy & Cole) house Elm near Main
" Maud M. teacher piano-forte, house George S. do.
" Rebecca F. house George S. do.
" Roscoe K. carpenter, house Brook
Coleman Walter H. supt. Electric Light Co. house Railroad near Electric Light Works
Collins Bridget Mrs. (Dennis) house High n. No. Andover road
" Cornelius, coachman P. D. Smith, house Cornelius A. do.
" Cornelius A. laborer, h. North Main n. railroad bridge
" Daniel, laborer, house foot Morton
" Daniel, emp. Tyer Rubber Co. house Mrs. Ellen Haley
" John, emp. Joseph Smith, house 123 Main, F. V.
" John, house Ballard Vale
" John, plumber, house Daniel do.
" John A. emp. Smith & Dove, house Maurice do.
" John O. teamster, house Pearson
" M. Joseph, house Maurice do.
" Mary E. dressmaker, house Maurice do.
" Maurice, engineer, house Summer
" Nellie, domestic, house Miss Mary A. Ballard
" Thomas, house Ballard Vale
Colpitts Victoria L. house Mrs. Mary E. Kimball
Colquhoun John H. hosiery mfr. B. V. h. n. the church, W. P.
Colts Asa, emp. Bradlee mill, boards Mrs. Caroline Walker
Comerford Mary E. house William D. Stark
Comiskey Martin, emp. C. & K. house River, B. V.
Conley John, emp. Stevens mill, house Marland, M. V.
" Hannah Mrs. house Marland, M. V.
" Timothy, boards Mrs. Hannah do.
Connell James E. farmer, house Boston road, B. V.
" Mary, house 8 Brick block, A. V.
Connelly John T. laborer, house Morton
" Thomas J. emp. Stevens mill, house Marland, M. V.
Connors James, house Center District
" Peter, house Village District
Conway Catherine Mrs. (Thomas) house Andover, B. V.
" John T. house Ballard Vale
" Patrick, night watchman Bradlee mills, h. Centre, B. V.
Copeland Rubina, teacher, boards Mrs. Catherine Mears
Coston Albert, house Center District
Cotter James, house Ballard Vale
" Julia Mrs. (James) house John P. Driscoll
Cottrell William, house Bailey District
Coulie Emilie B. Mrs. (James L.) house Alms, F. V.
" James L. house Frye Village
" Lyall H. plumber, house Mrs. Emily B. do.

Coutts William C. overseer Smith & Dove, house Cuba
Cox Arthur W. last maker, house Summer
Coyle Peter, blacksmith, house River, B. V.
Craig George, house Lowell, F. V.
Craik James, boot and shoe repairer, Mineral n. Village, h. do.
Cram Lemuel P. machinist, house Oak, B. V.
Cranz C. Albert, emp. C. & K. house Andover, B. V.
Cronin Cornelius, emp. C. & K. house Lowell, B. V.
" Daniel, emp. Moses White, boards Dennis J. Carey
" Jeremiah, section man B. & M. R. R. h. Centre, B. V.
Cropley William W. farmer, house Salem, P. D.
Cross John, laborer, house Caldwell farm, off Main, S. D.
" Willard, agent, boards Miss Mary W. Towne
Crowley Delia Mrs. house Mrs. Ellen do.
" Ellen Mrs. (Cornelius) house North Main n. the bridge
" James, house North District
" Michael J. emp. P. J. Hannon, house Mrs. Ellen do.
" William C. clerk A. Bliss, house Mrs. Ellen do.
Crowninshield John C. house School near Main
Cullen Michael, house Andover, B. V.
Cullinane Jeremiah, section hand B. & M. R. R. house Ridge
Cummings Aaron, farmer, house Phillips
" Annie Mrs. (Joseph) house Mrs. Sarah Priest
" Arthur G. student, house Aaron do.
CUMMINGS BRAINARD, contractor and builder, Park, house Punchard av. c. Park
CUMMINGS CHARLES O. real estate, house Elm c. Washington av.
" Daniel, dealer in nursery stock, house 52 Salem, P. D.
" George, carpenter, house Washington av.
" John, house River, B. V.
" Lois M. house Aaron do.
Cunningham Adelia Mrs. house William Jackson
" David, emp. Stevens mill, house West Parish
" Frank, house North District
" Henry J. laborer, house Hugh do.
" Henry W. laborer, house rear Punchard school house
" Hugh, house Highland road near Salem
" Hugh J. emp. Fred M. Hill, h. Highland road off Salem
" Nellie M. house Hugh do.
" Peter F. bookkeeper, house Hugh do.
Curley Delia, domestic, house Edward B. Hutchinson
Curtis Carrie E. house Main, S. D.
Cushing Deborah Mrs. (George A.) house W. Byron Morse
Cuthbert David, emp. Tyer Rubber Co. house Cuba
Cutler Albalino B. farmer, house West Center District
" Granville, house West Center District
" William B. house West Center District

D

DAHL LOUIS, tailor, house Maple av.
Daly C. Julia, bookkeeper P. J. Daly, house do.
" Daniel, house North Main near the bridge
" Edward B. emp. C. & K. house Centre, B. V.
" James E. foreman Tyer Rubber Co. house Bartlet c. Chestnut
" Jeremiah J. clerk P. J. Daly, house Patrick J. do.
" Thomas, spinner, house River, B. V.
" Mary Mrs. house Nathan Ellis
" Michael J. hack, livery and boarding stable, boards Central Street Dining Room
" Patrick, emp. Frank E. Gleason, house North Main near the bridge

DALY PATRICK J. dry goods, groceries, etc. Elm square, house do.
" Thomas, Jr. buffer C. & K. house Thomas do.
" Thomas F. printer, boards Elm House
Dane Alice A. Mrs. (Henry) h. North Main n. railroad bridge
" George, farmer, house West Center District
" George A. farmer, house near Tewksbury line, O. D.
" Louis A. printer, house Mrs. Alice A. do.
" William F. house West Center District
Danneby John, section hand B. & M. R. R. house Baker's lane
Davey John, switchman B. & M. R. R. at Lowell Junction, house Marland c. Tewksbury, B. V.
" Patrick Mrs. house John do.
David Thomas, emp. Smith & Dove, house 123 Main, F. V.
Davis Abbie R. W. Mrs. (William W.) h. Bartlett n. Chestnut
" Abbie S. house Mrs. Mary A. do.
" Augustus M. painter, house 50 Salem, P. D.
" Charles E. printer, B. house Lowell, B. V.
" Elmer E. emp. Stevens mill, h. Harding c. North Main
" Frank A. carpenter, house Main junc. Porter
" Fred A. emp. trustees' farm, house 50 Salem, P. D.

DAVIS GEORGE E. painter and paper hanger, house 50 Salem, P. D.
" Lewis M. clerk J. H. Campion, house 50 Salem, P. D.
" Mary A. Mrs. (Warren) house Main c. Chestnut
Dawson Rebecca Mrs. house River, B. V.
Dean Alice C. house Mrs. Caroline L. do.
" Carrie A. teacher, house Mrs. Caroline L. do.
" Caroline L. Mrs. (John H.) house 54 Main
" George M. clerk G. H. Parker, h. Mrs. Caroline L. do.
" Hattie L. house Mrs. Caroline L. do.

Dean John W. merchant tailor, ready-made clothing, furnishings, etc. Main, house 54 Main near Chestnut
Dear Alexander, farmer, house off Salem, H. D.
Dearborn James, painter, house Porter, P. D.
" James E. house Ballard Vale
" John S. painter and paper hanger, house Andover, B. V.
" Lauren F. carpenter, house Elm near Washington av.
" Moses M. shoemaker, house off Main, S. D.
Delaney Robert, flax dresser, boards John Stack, Jr.
DeLorey Annie, boards J. Henry Allican
Dennehy Nellie, domestic, house Miss Dora S. Berry
Dennison James E. commercial salesman, house High
" Joseph A. house Main
" Mary A. Mrs. (John) house North Main
Derrah Alexander, supt. Shawsheen grove, h. foot Centre, B. V.
Desmond John, Jr. house Maple av.
Devitt Mary Mrs. (John P.) house Mrs. Richard J. Sherry
Devlin Peter, milk dealer, house river road, W. P.
Dick Alexander, flax dresser, house Mineral
" Alexander L. emp. Smith & Dove, house Essex, A. V.
Dimock Lydia, domestic, house F. E. Gleason
Dinsmore Austin H. upholsterer, house Frank A. do.
" Frank A. prop. Andover Steam Laundry, upholstering, etc. Park, house do.
" Lorin A. teamster, boards Wendell P. Jenkins
Disbrow Edward D. Rev. house Porter, P. D.
Dixon Allan, house Osgood District
" Thomas, house Osgood District
Doble Silas C. farmer, house Union near Lawrence line, F. V.
Dodge Frank E. house Center District
Dodson Charles, clerk Lawrence Hardware Co. h. High, F. V.
" Richard J. farmer and milkman, house High, F. V.
Doherty John F. emp. Sullivan & Willard, Lawrence, house Mrs. Margaret do.
" Margaret Mrs. (John) house Harding near High
" William J. carpenter, house Mrs. Margaret do.
Dole Georgiana C. Mrs. house off Salem, H. D.
" Sarah A. house Brainard Cummings
Donahue Maurice J. emp. B. & M. car shop, house Main, F. V.
Donald Alice D. house William C. do.
" Walter S. ink mfr. house Main near Union, F. V.
" William C. house Main, F. V.
Donnelly Sarah, domestic, house Nathan Ellis
Donohue James, emp. M. E. White, boards do.
" Mary Mrs. (Owen) house Oak, B. V.
" Sarah, house Oak, B. V.
Donovan Charles E. painter, house East Chestnut

Donovan Daniel, painter, house Pearson
" Daniel, stone mason, house Pearson
" Dennis, house Brook c. Essex
" Dennis, 2d, plasterer, house North Main c. Harding
" James, farmer, house Salem, H. D.
" James A. laborer, house North Main
" James A. express messenger, house Daniel do.
" Jennie, house Peter D. Smith
" John, plasterer, house Ridge
" John F. machinist, house Daniel do.
" Katie, domestic, house George Gould
" Katie E. dressmaker, house Dennis do.
" Maggie E. house Daniel do.
" Margaret C. teacher, house Dennis do.
" Mary A. house Dennis do.
" Mary T. house Peter D. Smith
" Patrick, section foreman B. & M. R. R. h. Marland, B V.
" Patrick, laborer, house Baker's lane
" Peter J. coachman, house Dennis do.
Dow Elizabeth, house Main near Porter
Downs Samuel M. Prof. music teacher, h. Main n. Punchard av.
Downing Emanuel, farmer, house Mrs. John do.
" John Mrs. house Highland road n. North Andover line
Dove George W. W. (Smith & Dove, shoe thread mfrs.) house Main, F. V.
" John, house George W. W. do.
Doyle George A. house West Center District
" Maggie Mrs. domestic, house Mrs. Susan B. Chadwick
" Thomas E. emp. Stevens mill, boards John McCallion
Draper Warren F. publisher of theological works, house School
Drinkwater Julia A. Mrs. (Arthur) house 71 Main
Driscoll Dennis P. laborer, house Harding n. the railroad bridge
" John D. stone mason, house Summer
" John J. clerk J. M. Bradley, house Pearson
" John P. laborer, house Harding near railroad bridge
" Patrick, night watchman Tyer Rubber Co. house School c. Ridge
Dubold John F. house Phillips District
Duffee John, emp. Stevens mill, house Marland, M. V.
Duffley Barney F. emp. Matthew Kelley, house do.
Dugan Martin, house Center District
" Peter, house Center District
Dugdale James E. emp. C. & K. house Oak, B. V.
Dumphie Peter, house Osgood District
Duncan Charles J. house Mrs. Ann Saunders
" Margaret Mrs. (Robert) house Mrs. Ann Saunders
" Mary E. house Mrs. Katherine A. Paine

Dundas William, tailor, house Essex c. Baker's lane
Dunigan Bridget, house Brick block, A. V.
Dunnels George C. house Maple av. c. Walnut av.
Dunsheath Euphemie Mrs. (Samuel) house River, B. V.
Duren Mabel, house Miss Philena McKeen
" Fanny, house Miss Philena McKeen
Durning Margaret, domestic, house Rev. Edward W. Pride
Duval Isabel Mrs. (Pierre) house Cuba junc. Mineral
" Euphemia I. typewriter, house Mrs. Isabel do.
" Jules A. emp. Tyer Rubber Co. house Mrs. Isabel do.
Dwane Mary Mrs. (John) house Dean's block, Main
" Mary Mrs. (Daniel) house Morton
" Margaret, house Mrs. Mary do.
Dwyer John J. house Ballard Vale
" William, house Ballard Vale .

E

EAMES LEMUEL H. meat and provisions, house Elm c. Maple av.
" Plato, farmer, house Elm
" Sophronia O. Mrs. (Jonathan) house Lemuel H. do.
Eastman Charles B. carpenter, house 35 Salem, P. D.
" Eben R. barber, house East Chestnut
" Ira A. boarding house for students of Phillips Academy, house Porter
Eastwood David C. spinner, house Marland, M. V.
" Reuben, spinner, house North Main near Harding
Eaton Abbie P. soprano soloist, house Joshua P. do.
" George T. instructor at Phillips Academy, house Bartlet near Wheeler
" Horace P. baggage master O. C. R. R. h. Village, A. V.
" James A. clerk, house Cuba
" Joshua P. shoe mfr. house Central opp. Brook
" Lyman W. house Ballard Vale
" Walter H. clerk A. Bliss, house Maple av.
Eck Peter, emp. C. & K. house Davis block, Centre, B. V.
Edwards Clarence E. house Abbot District
" Henry, mfr. machine brushes, house river road, W. P.
Ellis Ellen G. house Nathan do.
" Nathan, academy boarding house, house Main c. Morton
Emerson Eliza A. W. Mrs. house Jabez Wardman
" Hovey, shoemaker, h. Main n. North Reading line, S. D.
English Patrick, blacksmith, house High near No. Andover road
Erving Abbott, janitor grammar school building, h. Salem, P. D.
" Hattie, house Mrs. Joanna do.
" Joanna Mrs. house Salem, P. D.

Evans John C. Rev. pastor Union Cong. church, B. V. house Village c. Centre, B. V.
Ewing George, fireman Bradlee mill, house Andover, B. V.

F

Fagan Lawrence, house B. V.
Fallows John, emp. Bradlee mills, house Marland, B. V.
" John Jr. emp. C. & K. house John do.
Farmer Everett W. clerk Charlestown Five Cent Savings bank, house Thomas J. do.
" Herbert R. house Thomas J. do.
" Nellie, bookkeeper John N. Cole, house Thomas J. do.
FARMER T. J. fish, oysters, etc. Post-office av. house 40 Punchard av.
Farnham Emeline H. Mrs. (Charles) house Joshua H. Stott
" Ezra, house off Mineral n. railroad bridge, W. C.
" Moses L. clerk Smith & Manning, house High
Feeney James J. clerk Smith & Manning, house Michael do.
" Michael, farmer, house off Salem, H. D.
Fessenden Edmund M. organist and musical director, house Mrs. Mary A. do.
" George M. modeler and designer, house Mrs. Mary A. do.
" Mary A. Mrs. (Edmund M.) house Andover, B. V.
Fickert Richard, machinist, house Oak, B. V.
Field Joseph, farmer, house Lowell, O. D.
Fielding Fred, house North Main near Harding
Filtan John, house Haverhill
Findley Richard M. emp. Tyer Rubber Co. house Maple av. near Walnut av.
" William F. emp. Tyer Rubber Co. house Summer
Finlay Ellen, domestic, house Theodore C. Pease
Finn William, emp. Bradlee mill, house Centre, B. V.
Fischer Charles A. H. emp. C. & K. house Chester, B. V.
Fisher Amelia B. house William B. Wood
Fiske Joseph B. clerk J. E. Sears, boards Central Street Dining Room
" Harry, emp. Tyer Rubber Co. boards Frank B. Jenkins
Fitzgerald Thomas, farmer, h. off river road, W. A. station, A. D.
" Timothy, clerk J. H. Campion, rooms Edward Trefry
Fitzpatrick Daniel, farmer, house off river road, W. A. station, A. D.
Flagg Hannah Mrs. house Main near Porter
Flaherty Hugh, emp. Bradlee mill, house River, B. V.
" Kate, house Hugh do.
" Mary V. weaver, house Hugh do.
" Michael, emp. C. & K. house Hugh do.

Flaherty Nellie, weaver, house Hugh do.
Flanders Eliza R. Mrs. (Lucien B.) boards Benjamin Brown
Flemming Eliza Mrs. emp. Smith & Dove, house Mineral near Village
Flint Charles H. farmer, house Lowell, O. D.
" George E. farmer, house off Salem, Jenkins Corner, H. D.
" George E. 2d, farmer, house B. D.
" Hannah Mrs. (Alanson) house Henry K. do.
" Henry K. farmer, house Lowell road, O. D.
" James S. farmer, house Bailey District

FLINT JOHN H. treas. Tyer Rubber Co. house Elm c. High

" Joshua, house Abbot District
" Maria H. house Henry K. do.
" Nathaniel F. house High
Flynn William E. emp. Stevens mill, house Marland, M. V.
Follansbee John, farmer, house Andover, Haggett's pond, W. P.
" Paul B. nurseryman, h. Andover, Haggett's pond, W. P.
Ford Isabella Mrs. (James) house Main near Porter
Fortis John, house Frye Village
" S. Annie, dressmaker, house William H. do.
" William H. teamster Smith & Dove, house Lowell, F. V.
Forsyth Catherine Mrs. house Marland, M. V.
Foster Alfred, emp. H. P. Noyes, boards Charles E. Torrey
" Anna Mrs. (William P.) house 51 Central
" Carrie M. house Mrs. Rhoda J. do.
" Ella H. house Mrs. Rhoda J. do.
" Elmira Mrs. house Main near Morton
" Francis Homer, house 51 Central
" Frank M. farmer, house Porter, P. D.
" Frederick, upholsterer, house No. Main n. Tyer Rubber Co.
" George C. milk dealer, house 32 Salem, P. D.

FOSTER GEORGE W. counsellor at law, office Bank building, Main, office hours 8 to 12 a. m. and 2 to 5 p. m., house Main

Foster Mary Mrs. (Thomas) house Jacob W. Barnard
FOSTER MOSES, cashier Andover National bank and president Andover Savings bank, house Elm
" Rhoda J. Mrs. (William H.) house 32 Salem, P. D.
Fraser James, machinist, house Poor, F. V.
" John, hairdresser, boards Mrs. Bessie R. Hill
" John, emp. Tyer Rubber Co. house Mineral near the bridge, A. V.
" Stewart, emp. Smith & Dove, bds. Mrs. Mary McIntosh
Frederickson August, emp. William M. Wood, house do.
Freeman Missouri, domestic, house George H. Poor
French Lucy A. house Main c. Morton
" Jonathan, house Main c. Morton
Frosch Bernard, house Ballard Vale
" William, machinist, house Lowell, B. V.
Frye Charles H. house High near Elm square
" Eliza Mrs. (George) house William L do.
" Laura A. house Charles H. do.
" William L. baggage master B. & M. R. R. house East Chestnut near Bartlet
Fryer John, plumber, house Washington av.
Fuller William F. house W. D.

G

GALVIN JOHN J. house Mrs. Mary do.
" Mary Mrs. (Patrick) house Chester, B. V.
" William P. laborer, house Mrs. Mary do.
Gannon Linda Mrs. (William) house Blaney block, Andover, B.V.
Gardner Jennie Mrs. (Charles) house Anthony Ward
" H. J. station agent Lowell Junc., house Andover, B. V.
" S. M. H. Mrs. house Bartlet near Wheeler
Garside James, periodical store, South Boston, house No. Main
" John, spinner, house James do.
Gay Charles W. Mrs. house Mrs. Mary T. Wildes
Geagin Jennie, boards Charles E. Torrey
Gee Thomas, gardener, house Chester, B. V.
GEORGI THEODORE C. portrait artist, house Washington av. near Summer
Getchell Ella R. house James H. Cochrane
Gibbons Margaret, domestic, house Rev. John P. Gulliver
Gibbs Theodore A. shoemaker, house Oak, B. V.
Gibon Ellen, domestic, house Nathan Ellis
Gibson Rebecca R. Mrs. millinery, house Lowell, B. V.
Giddings H. E. Miss, house Chestnut near Main

GILBERT CHARLES H., M. D. S. dentist, dental rooms Bank building, Main. Office hours, 8 a. m. to 12 m., 1.30 to 5.30 p. m., house Main near Morton

" Guy W. student, house Charles H. do.
" Perley F. student, house Charles H. do.
Gile Erastus Mrs. house 52 North Main
" Georgiana, house 52 North Main
Gill John B. iron moulder, house Chester, B. V.
Gillespie William, house Main, F. V.
Gilman Harriet Mrs. house Phelps crossing, Haggett's pond
" Mary Mrs. (Enos S.) house Highland road near Salem
Gilson Albert A. laborer, house Caldwell farm, off Main, S. D.
Gleason Benjamin G. mason, house Lowell near church, W. P.
" Eliza, bookkeeper F. E. Gleason, house do.

GLEASON FRANK E. coal, wood, etc. Main, house 15 High

" James, emp. B. B. Tuttle, house Lowell, W. P.
" Moses V. mason and builder, Maple av. house do.

GLEASON NESBIT G. agent American Express, office Elm square, boards Mary H. Grosvenor

Gledhill William F. emp. Smith & Manning, house Marland, M.V.
Glidden Jane A. dressmaker, rooms William G. Brown
Glispin John, house Center District
Goff Fred B. clerk Howard National Bank, Boston, house Mrs. Martha P. do.
" Herbert, emp. Union Pacific R. R., B. house Mrs. Martha P. do.
" Martha P. Mrs. (Henry) house High
" William H. emp. electric light station, house Mrs. Martha P. do.
Golding Jeremiah, house Abbot District
Goldsmith Clarence, student, house William G. do.
" Elizabeth G. Mrs. (Jeremiah) house William G. do.
" George, house West Center District
" James H. carpenter, house off Main, S. D.
" Joseph C. shoemaker, house off Main, S. D.
" Phebe Mrs. (Joseph C.) house James H. do.
" William G. postmaster, house Elm near Maple av.
Goldthwaite Ida G. teacher, boards Hezekiah Jones

Goodell Calvin E. boards Moses L. Farnham
Goodwin Charles H. emp. C. & K. house High, B. V.
" David, laborer, house Pearson
" Frank R. emp. A. W. W. house David do.
" George S. emp. Frank Gleason, house David do.
" Sherman, foreman stock room C. & K. house Charles H. do.
" Sylvester, teamster, house Pearson
" William H. station agent, house Summer
" Winslow, purchasing agent C. & K. house Charles H. do.
Gordon John, emp. Smith & Dove, house Village near Cuba
Gorst Joseph, laborer, house Tewksbury road, O. D.
Gosselin Allen, telegraph operator, boards Mrs. Bessie R. Hill
Gould Charles B. Mrs. house 27 Salem
" George, stock broker, Boston, house Main near Porter
" Henry A. farmer, house off Main, near No. Reading line
" Henry E. farmer, house Main, S. D.
" Julia, house George do.
" Mary B. Mrs. house George do.
" Milo H. farmer, house Henry A. do.
Graffam George H. farmer, house Porter
Graham Charles S. emp. electric light station, house Freeman R. Abbott
" Hannah Mrs. (John) house 54 North Main
" Mary E. house Mrs. Hannah do.
Grandy Frank A. emp. C. & K. boards James Hudson, Jr.
Graves William B. Prof. professor in Phillips Academy, house Salem near Main
Gray Alice, house Henry do.
" Henry, farmer, house Salem, H. D.
" Ira O. carpenter, house Kimball House, Elm
" Margaret E. house Central near Main
" Sophronia A. Mrs. (David) house 6 Chestnut
" Thomas E. laborer, house Prospect near Prospect Hill
" Walter E. printer, house William H. do.
" William H. printer, house 63 Salem, H. D.
GREENE CHARLES, (Greene & Woodlin) grocers, Ballard Vale, house Centre, B. V.
" Frederick W. Rev. pastor West Congregational Church, house near the Church, W. P. Dist.
" Jessie F. teacher, house William H. do.
" John, house Osgood Dist.
" William H. clerk Greene & Woodlin, house Lowell cor. Chester, B. V.
Greenough Mary Mrs. house Miss Charlotte S. Abbott
Greenwood John, emp. Bradlee mill, house foot Sand, B. V.
" Robert H. house Osgood Dist.
" William, spinner Bradlee mill, house Sand, B. V.

Greig William, night watchman Smith & Dove, house Mineral
Gribbin J. R. bookbinder, house 33 Salem, P. D.
Griffin Maria, house 52 Main
Grosvenor James, house Maple av. c. Walnut av.
" Mary H. house Essex

GRUBER C. F. prop. Elm House, Main c. Elm, house do.

Gulliver John Francis, counsellor-at-law, house Rev. John Putnam do.
" John Putnam Rev. prof. in Theological Seminary, house Main opp. Salem
Gunnison Abiah, tailoress, house 28 Essex
" Mary J. tailoress, house 28 Essex
Guthrie David P. emp. Smith & Dove, house foot Essex
Gutterson Myron E. junk dealer, house Maple av. near Elm

H

Haber Paul, emp. C. & K. house Andover, B. V.
Hackett Albert W. farmer, house William do.
" Edward F. farmer, house William do.
" William, farmer, house Main, S. D.
" William H. farmer, house Main, S. D.
Hadden William, flaxdresser, house Village n. the bridge, A. V.
Haggerty James, stone mason, h. North Main, n. railroad bridge
" John A. emp. C. & K. house River, B. V.
" Timothy, laborer, house foot Morton
" Timothy J. emp. C. & K. house Ballard Vale
" William J. iceman, house off Main, S. D.
Haigh Thomas, house Bailey District
" William A. house West Parish
Haley Ellen Mrs. house North Main near the bridge
" Mary Mrs. house River, B. V.
Hall Mary D. Mrs. (Rev. Alfred H.) house East Chestnut
Halpen Michael J. house Abbot Dist.
Hammel Alexander, house Centre Dist.
Hamilton John, house B. V.
Hammond Amon F. emp. Tyer Rubber Co. house Park, opp. Bartlet
" Schuyler, house Ballard Vale
Handy Elizabeth L. house Main near Morton
" John L. Mrs. house Main near Morton
Hanford Mary A. C. Mrs. (Albert G.) house Prof. George F. Moore
Hannon Bridget Mrs. (Patrick) house Florence
" Kate, domestic, house Miss Abbie H. Peabody
" Margaret Mrs. (Stephen) house North Main

HANNON P. J. tailor and men's furnisher, Main, house Florence
Hanson Eugene A. clerk Valpey Bros. house Center District
" Sylvester W. farmer, house river road, W. P.
Hardy Albert A. farmer, house river road, W. P.
" Charles A. mfr. machine brushes, house Lowell, W. P.
" Edward S. farmer, house Bailey District
" Elbridge G. farmer, house river road, W. P.
" Frank H. brushmaker, boards Charles A. do.
" Frederick L. farmer, house Bailey District
" George A. farmer, house Bailey District
" Harrison H. farmer, house Bailey District
" Lewis T. (Hardy & Cole) box mfrs. carpenters and builders, house Maple av.
" Maria Mrs. house Lowell, F. V.
" Stephen, house Bailey District
Harnden George W. proprietor Harnden farm, house Salem, H. D.
" John S. emp. Tyer Co. house Harding cor. No. Main
" Stillman H. carpenter, house 26 Essex
Harnedy William, teamster, house Pearson
Harnett Frank, house Ballard Vale
Harraden William C. clerk Smith & Manning, boards Mrs. Mary A. Davis
Harrell Eleanora, domestic, house James B. Smith
" Emma, house John L. Smith
" Sarah E. domestic, house J. Warren Berry
Harrigan Dennis, house Centre District
HARRIMAN THOMAS P. horseshoer, wheelwright and general blacksmith, Park, house Elm
Harrington Daniel F..farmer, house Osgood District
" Daniel J. emp. Tyer Rubber Co. boards Michael J. Maroney
Harris Ellison T. house Ballard Vale
" Emma, emp. Smith & Dove, boards William Johnston
" George Rev. professor in Theolgical Seminary, house Main near Porter
" John S. emp. Smith & Dove, house Essex corner Baker's lane
" Samuel R. emp. Smith & Dove, boards Mrs. Ann Higginbottom
Harrison Benjamin. engineer, house Andover, B. V.
" Peter, house Maple av.
" Sarah A. Mrs. house Sand, B. V.
Harrold James, coachman W. M. Wood, house Main, F. V.
Hart Daniel, laborer, house Cuba
" Ellen, house Dr. Cecil F. P. Bancroft
" Hannah, house Miss Mary K. Roberts

Hart John, emp. Smith & Dove, house 1 Brick block, A. V.
Hartigan David, house No. Main, near the bridge
Hartley William P. emp. Tyer Rubber Co. h. Central n. Main
Harvey James, house 1 Brick block, A. V.
" Rosanna, house James do.
Haskell Byron A. house Center District
" Clarence M. carpenter, house off Main, P. D.
" Richard, carpenter, house Clarence M. do.
Hastings Annie, emp. Smith & Dove, boards Thomas W. Wilkie
" Catherine, emp. Smith & Dove, bds. Thomas W. Wilkie
Haupert David M. carriage painter, house Jacob J. do
" Jacob J. emp. Smith & Dove, house Main, F. V.
Hax John, emp. C. & K. house Marland block, Centre, B. V.
Hayes Elizabeth Mrs. (James) house Main c. Lowell, F. V.
" George, house Frye Village
" Maggie, house Rev. John Phelps Taylor
Haynes Bancroft T. (F. G. Haynes & Co.) dry goods, groceries, etc. Andover c. River, B. V. house Tewksbury, B. V.
" Felix G. house Ballard Vale
Hayward Carrie P. cashier Arlington Co-operative Store, Lawrence, house Henry A. do.
" Edward G. mariner, house Henry M. do.
" Gertrude A. dressmaker, house Henry A. do.
" George H. civil engineer and surveyor, h. Henry A. do.
" Harriet E. house 27 School
" Henry A. farmer, house Porter, P. D.

HAYWARD HENRY M. coal, wood, lumber and ice, yard High, B. V. house do.
" Polly S. Mrs. (Henry E.) house 27 School
" Walter A. farmer, house off Central near railroad
Hazelwood Webster, commercial salesman, house Punchard av. near Main
Hefferan Martin, emp. Bradlee mill, house Centre, B. V.
Heffernan Michael, laborer, boards Nelson E. Maskell
Hemenway Charles O. assistant sexton Episcopal church, house foot Abbot
Henabry Ambrose, emp. C. & K. house Chester, B. V.
Henderson Charles, house West Dist.
" George N. emp. Hardy & Cole, house Cuba
" John, carpenter, house Mineral
" John M. watchman Smith & Dove, house Lowell corner Main, F. V.
" John W. house Abbot District
Hendrickson John, farmer, house Boston road, B. V.
Herrick Franklin H. foreman Bradlee mill, house Tewksbury, B. V.
" George W. jeweler, house Franklin H. do.
" Mary E. Mrs. (Charles) house Marland, B. V.

Hibbert Nelson C. house North District
Hickey John, section foreman B. & M. R. R. house Mineral
" Timothy, section hand B. & M. R. R. house Mineral
Hidden D. I. C. farmer, house So. Main near junction Main
Higginbottom Ann Mrs. house No. Main
" George, emp. Stevens mill, boards Mrs. Ann do.
Higgins Anna O. house Mrs. Sarah A. do.
" Annie, house Joseph W. do.
" Charles A. foreman Elm House stables, house Henry C. do.
" Frank P. bookkeeper Valpey Bros. house Henry C. do.
" George A. local editor Andover Townsman, house Henry C. do.
" Henry C. house Morton near Bartlet
" John W. emp. Tyer Rubber Co. boards Joseph W. do.
" Joseph W. conductor E. R. R. house Essex n. railroad
" Mary A. house 42 Central
" Sarah A. Mrs. (James H.) house High
" Sarah E. house Mrs. Sarah A. do.

HIGGINS WILLIAM H. proprietor Elm House Livery stables, Elm square, boards Mrs. Charlotte Barnett

Hill Alfred H. milk dealer, house Lowell junction
" Bessie R. Mrs. (Robert) house High
" Etta J. Mrs. (George) house Summer
" Fred M. superintendent seminary and academy grounds and buildings, house Chapel av.
" Henry A. painter, house Poor, F. V.
" John, machinist, house Haverhill, F. V.
" Lucy E. R. Mrs. (George W. R.) house Main c. Morton
" Marcus M. hotel clerk, house Haverhill, F. V.
Hilton Daniel C. cloth finisher, house Henry do.
" Henry, spinner, house North Main
" John, in Summer, house Lowell, O. D.
" Jonathan, emp. Tyer Rubber Co. house Henry do.
" Joseph, woolen twister, house Henry do.
Hinchcliffe Jonathan B. dresser Bradlee mill, house Joseph do.
" Joseph, dresser Bradlee mill, house Sand, B. V.
Hincks Edward Y. Rev. prof. in Andover Theological Seminary, house Bartlet near Morton
Hinton Allen, ice cream mfr. house South Main, S. D.
" Edward R. house Allen do.
Hirst Joshua, emp. Stevens mill, house North Main near Simpson's bridge
Hitchcock Elisha P. prop. Mansion House, Chapel av. house do.
" Elisha P. Mrs. house Phillips near Phillips Academy
" George P. house Mansion House
" L. P. gardener, house off Central near railroad
Hobbs Augustus, carpenter and builder, house Main, F. V.

Hodgdon Thomas A. Rev. pastor Methodist Episcopal church, B. V. house Tewksbury, B. V.
Hodge Alexander, emp. Robert Hodge, boards Robert do.
" Janet, house Robert do.
" Robert, proprietor Andover Bakery, Park, house do.

HODGES AMY M. MRS. proprietor American Hand Laundry, Main, house do.
" Frank, emp. Thomas Farmer, house Maple av.
" Samuel L. house Centre District
Hodnett Patrick, laborer, house No. Main, near the bridge
Hoffman Carl, emp. C. & K. boards Edgar F. Sisco
Hoffmann Emil P. machinist, house foot Centre, B. V.
Holden Walker, janitor Phillips Academy, house 23 Salem
" William, janitor Theological Seminary, house 23 Salem
Holland Mary Mrs. house John J. Buckley
Holmes Nellie, house William Shaw
" Joseph, house Frye Village
" Thomas F. house Lowell, F. V.
Horan Patrick, emp. Bradlee mill, house Oak, B. V.
" Thomas, emp. C. & K. house Patrick do.
" William, emp. Bradlee mill, house River, B. V.
Holroyd Mary Mrs. (John) house Centre, B. V.
" Mary J. house Warren Mears
Holt Ballard, librarian Public Library, house Maple av.
" Brooks F. ice dealer, house Main, S. D.
" E. Francis, superintendent of grounds of Abbot Academy, house Abbot near School
" Ellen A. house Brainard Cummings
" Etta, teacher, house Mrs. Susan M. do.
" Frank L. clerk Valpey Bros. house Mrs. Susan M. do.
" George A. carpenter, house Main corner Chestnut
" George E. clerk T. A. Holt & Co. house Mrs. Susan M. do.
" George F. house West Center District
" John M. house Elm, near North Andover line
" John V. clerk Howard Nat. Bank, Boston, h. Ballard do.
" Lizzie, dressmaker, house Marcus M. do.
" Marcus M. farmer, house Main, P. D.
" Maurice G. carpenter, boards L. H. Eames
" P. Elizabeth, house E. Francis do.
" Robert W. house West Center
" Samuel B. carpenter, house 6 Chestnut
" Sarah Mrs. (Deane) house Ballard do.
" Susan M. Mrs. (Warren E.) house Punchard av. n. Park

HOLT T. A. dry goods, groceries, etc. Central, boards Mrs. Betsey Abbott
" Timandra, house Marcus M. do.
Hovey John C. farmer, house off Main, S. D.

Howard Hannah, dressmaker, house Timothy do.
" Henry P. mason, house Post-Office av.
" M. J. Miss, millinery and dressmaking Post-Office av. house 42 Main
" Timothy, stone mason, house No. Main, n. railroad bridge
" William F. clerk J. H. Campion, house Timothy do.
Howarth Edward, foreman Stevens mills, house No. Main, near Marland
" Mary E. domestic, house Mrs. Betsey Abbott
" Nellie, house Centre, B. V.
" Oberlin B. carpenter, house near Smith & Dove office
" Sarah F. F. Mrs. (Dr. James) house near Smith & Dove office
Howe Sarah J. Mrs. (Niles) house John Howell
HOWELL JOHN, (Stickney & Howell) carpenter and builder, house Summer near Punchard av.
Hoyt George Mrs. house Mrs. Frances A. Whipple
Hudson James, spinner, house Sand, B. V.
" James Jr. woolsorter, house Andover, B. V.
Hughes George, emp. Stevens mills, boards Charles E. Torrey
Hull James, foreman Smith & Dove, house Essex
" James D. shoe packer, house James do.
" Margaret E. clerk Stevens mill, house James do.
HULME ALBERT E., D. M. D. dentist, office over J. H. Chandler's, Main, house Brook
" Frederick, foreman Tyer Rubber Co. house Brook
Hunt James W. sexton Cong. church, W. C. house Lowell, W. P.
" Mary, house Lowell, W. P.
Hunter Ann Mrs. house Mineral
" Maggie, emp. Smith & Dove, house William do.
" Margaret C. house Rev. Henry R. Wilbur
" William, house Village, A. V.
Hurley Daniel A. shipping clerk, house John do.
" John, fireman Hardy & Cole, house Harding near railroad bridge
" John F. carpenter, house John do.
" Mary A. seamstress, house John do.
" Randall, emp. A. W. W. boards Daniel Sheehan
Hussey Charles G. sawmill, house Chestnut, near Central
" George E. engraver, house Charles G. do.
Hutcheson John E. fish dealer, Main, house Summer, near North Andover line
Hutchinson Charles, house Bailey District
" Edward B. house Punchard av. corner Bartlet
" Ella D. Mrs. (Homer) house 60 Salem, H. D.

J

JACKSON CAROLINE R. MRS. house Abbott near Phillips
" Caleb, house West District
" Stephen, carpenter, house Maple av.
" Susanna E. house Abbot, near Phillips
" William T. leather dealer, 242 Purchase street, Boston, house Abbot near School

Jameson Charles A. house West Center District
Jansen Benedicta, domestic, house William S. Jenkins
Jaquith M. Alice, teacher, house Newton do.
" Hannah A. house Morton near Main
" Henry A. shoe cutter, house Morton near Main
" Newton, shoe mfr. house Main, S. D.
" Newton, Jr. shoe cutter, house Mrs. Sarah A. Mason

Jarvie Margaret S. teacher piano-forte, house Abbot n. Phillips
Jenkins Alvin, house Salem, Jenkins' Corner, H. D.
" Charles B. bookkeeper T. A. Holt & Co. house Punchard av. c. Chestnut
" Edward S. house Center District
" Frank B. shipping clerk Tyer Rubber Co. house East Chestnut
" John B. farmer, house Salem, Jenkins' Corner, H. D.
" Kate P. house William S. do.
" Kendall E. county treasurer, house 29 School
" Omar, carpenter, house High
" Robert, house High
" Sally Mrs. (Ebenezer) house off Main, S. D.
" Sarah, house Mrs. Sally do.
" Stewart, clerk, house 29 School
" Wendell P. carpenter, house Elm, near Washington av.
" William S. president Merrimack Mutual Fire Ins. Co. house 69 Main

Jewett Charles H. foreman Stevens mills, house No. Main, near Harding
Johnson Charles H. engineer Electric Light Co. house High
" Francis H. Rev. house Elm, near Walnut av.
" Isaac, section foreman B. & M. R. R. boards Patrick Donovan
" James, section hand B. & M. R. R. boards Patrick Donovan
" James E. salesman, B. house Main near Locke
" Joseph, farmer, house 55 Salem, P. D.
" Lizzie A. Mrs. theological boarding house, house Bartlet c. Morton

Johnston William, laborer, house 14 Brick block, A. V.
Jones Anna E. house Louis H. Schneider

Jones Delina A. Mrs. (William T.) house Tewksbury, B. V.
" Edwin, shoe cutter, boards Mrs. Anna M. Woodbridge
" Frederick H. emp. Tyer Rubber Co. house S. D.
" Hezekiah, farmer, house South Main, S. D.
" Mary J. Mrs. (Charles E.) house 13 Essex
" Samuel M. milk dealer, house off Main, S. D.
" Susie, domestic, house James B. Smith
" Susie K. house Hezekiah do.
Jonson Gustave J. tailor, boards Elm House
Joslin Joseph J. house Ballard Vale
Jowett Charles H. house Center District
" John W. asst. supt. Stevens mill, house High n. Harding
" William H. supt. Stevens mill, h. Main n. railroad bridge
Joyce Catherine, house James do.
" James, house Andover, B. V.
" James, Jr. spinner, house James do.
" Maurice, house Ballard Vale
JOYCE PATRICK V. cigars, tobacco, confectionery, etc. Tewksbury, B. V. h. Andover, c. Tewksbury, B. V.
" Thomas J. spelter caster, house James do.

K

Kazer James A. upholsterer, bds. Central Street Dining Room
Keane Nellie, domestic, house Mrs. Lucia W. Merrill
Keefe James O. farmer, house Alms, F. V.
Keeland John E. house J. W. Wardwell
KEELAND JOHN E. cigars, confectionery, etc. Andover, B. V. house Lowell, B. V.
Kelesey Mary E. matron Smith Hall, house do.
Kelley Ellen, boards Joshua Hirst
" John, section hand B. & M. R. R. boards Michael McCormick
" Julia, boards Joshua Hirst
" Matthew, horse undertaker, house Union near Lawrence line, F. V.
Kendall Eliza A. Mrs. (Henry J.) house 6 Chestnut
" Frank H. E. carpenter, house 6 Chestnut
Kent Sarah, house George Dane
Kerr Elizabeth Mrs. (James) house River, B. V.
Kershaw John, house Brook near Central
Kibbee Charles H. farmer, house Lowell, B. V.
" James H. carpenter, house Lowell, B. V.
Killacky John, emp. Smith & Dove, house Marland, M. V.
Kimball Angelina, matron Draper Hall, house do.
" John F. treasurer and clerk Andover Savings Bank, house Central, corner School

Kimball John Tyler, clerk Andover National Bank, h. 88 Main
" Lucy J. house John F. do.
" M. Florence, asst. clerk Andover Savings Bank, house John F. do.
" Mary E. Mrs. (Dr. Walter H.) house School cor. Central
" Mary J. Mrs. (Thomas J.) house East Chestnut n. Main
King Patrick, emp. W. H. Higgins, house Pearson
Kinley Jesse Mrs. nurse, house Poor, F. V.
Kirby James, emp. Bradlee mill, house River, B. V.
Knight Charlotte Mrs. (James M.) house Mrs. Etta J. Hill
" Fenton A. hostler, house Isaac M. do.
" Frank H. expressman, house Daly block, No. Main
" Isaac M. foreman Thorndale Stables, house Elm near North Andover line
Knipe William, plumber, house No. Main, near Simpson bridge
" Wilson, emp. Stevens mill, house No. Main, near Simpson's bridge
Knowles Henrietta Mrs. house Main, near No. Reading line, S. D.
" Winslow L. book agent, house Mrs. Henrietta do.
Kydd Andrew, flax dresser, house Mineral, A. V.
" Eliza Mrs. house Mineral near the bridge, A. V.
" John, emp. Smith & Dove, house Village, opp. Cuba
" Thomas, machinist, house Main, F. V.

L

LADD FREDERICK H. student, house Mrs. Eliza D. do.
" Eliza D. Mrs. (John W.) house Main corner Chestnut
" Horace P. box manufacturer, house Marland, B. V.
" Tryphena W. Mrs. (Nathaniel) house Bartlet n. Chestnut
Laing David B. carpenter, house Lowell, F. V.
Lake George, house Village
Lamont Alexander, flax dresser, house Cuba, near Village
" Emma Mrs. (Alexander) house Central near Main
Lane Charles, emp. Bradlee mill, house Lowell, B. V.
" William, hostler, boards Isaac M. Knight
Lang Clara F. Mrs. (Dr. Ira M.) house 84 Main
" Herbert B. student, house 84 Main
Lange John, emp. C. & K., B. V. house Andover, B. V.
Langlands William, house Center District
Lassiter James H. coachman, house North Main c. Harding
" Willis P. janitor Barnard block, house do.
Latty William, house Village District
Laughlin Annie C. domestic, house Mrs. Julia A. Drinkwater
Laundry Anthoine, hostler, boards David Whitman

Lauster Paul, moulder C. & K. house Andover, B. V.
Law Edmund, emp. Stevens mill, house North Main n. Marland
Lawrence Fred, brass spinner C. & K. boards Mrs. May J. Parkhurst
" George F. polisher C. & K. house William do.
" Thomas A. W. plumber, house William do.
" William, laborer, house Chester, B. V.
Lawson Elizabeth Mrs. (George) house off Lowell near J. W. Mooar, W. P.
" George D. machinist, house Village opp. Cuba
" William S. house Elm
Leach Sanford H. house School opp. Abbot
Leahy Patrick, stone layer, house Pearson
Leary Jeremiah, laborer, house Morton
" John, laborer, house School
" John H. house Centre District
" William H. laborer, house School
Ledwell William T. billiard and pool room and hair-dresser, Park, boards Mrs. Bessie R. Hill
Leitch John A., M. D. physician and surgeon, office Barnard block, Main, house do.
" William, house Main, F. V.
Leslie David, flaxdresser, house Village near Cuba
" Thomas, laborer, house Mineral near Village, A. V.
" William Mrs. house Baker's lane
Lester Pharos R. house Center District
Lewis Joseph R. carpenter, house Washington av. near Elm
" Henry B., E. Frank Lewis, wool scouring mill, Lawrence, house Locke near Main
Libbey Annie Mrs. house Main near Morton
Lincoln Emma J. house Rev. Varnum do.
" Varnum Rev. house Summer near Punchard av.
Lindquist Axel, house Main c. Lowell, F. V.
" Carl, gardener W. M. Wood, house Main, F. V.
Lindsay Adam, foreman Smith & Dove. house Essex c. Pearson
" Annie Mrs. (James) house Mineral, A. V.
" Annie S. Mrs. (Alexander) house Mrs. Ann Saunders
" David S. clerk Valpey Bros. house Summer opp. Washington av.
" James, clerk Smith & Manning, house Robert do.
" John W. clerk Smith & Dove, house Walnut av.
" Robert, emp. Smith & Dove, house Lowell, F. V.
Linnehan Michael, laborer, house Tewksbury, B. V.
Livingston Charles W. house Osgood District
" Porter E. farmer, house Lowell, O. D.
" William, house Osgood District
Locke Annie L. house Samuel B. do.

Locke Florence M. teacher, house Samuel B. do.
" Marion, teacher, house Samuel B. do.
" Samuel B. iron founder, B. house Elm
Lockhart James, florist, High, boards Elm House
Long David, carpenter, house Harding c. North Main
Lord Mary Mrs. (George) house Marland, M. V.
" Mary Mrs. (Charles H.) h. Blaney blk. Andover, B. V.
" Turner H. laborer, house Central near Main
" William, house Center District
Loring Sarah A. M. Mrs. (John R.) house Abbot
Lovejoy Arthur, farmer, house Joseph T. do.
" Ballard, house Lowell, W. P.
" Fred, emp. Lawrence mill, house William do.
" George G. farmer, house Abbot District
" John T. farmer, house near Lowell, W. P.
" Joseph T. supt. of roads, house near Lowell, W. P.
" Stephen A. house Osgood District
" Sylvanus, farmer, house Lowell, O. D.
" Sylvester, house Osgood District
" William B. farmer, house Lowell, O. D.
" William W. farmer, house Lowell, W. P.
Low James, emp. Tyer Rubber Co. boards Elm House
Lowd Crosby W. expressman, house off Maple av.
" Joseph H. clerk T. A. Holt, house Maple av.
Lowe James C. foreman Smith & Dove, house opp. Smith & Dove's office
" Timothy, asst. road master B. & M. R. R. h. High, B. V.
" William H. emp. Stevens mill, house North Main near Simpson's bridge
Lunan William, emp. Smith & Dove. house Elm n. Walnut av.
Lundgren Martin, tailor, house School c. Ridge
Luscomb Alice, house Lowell, O. D.
" Annie, house Lowell, O. D.
Lynch John, laborer, house Morton
" John D. fruit dealer, house Morton
" Patrick, emp. C. & K. boards Mrs. Catherine Sherry
" P. A. Rev. curate, house Rev. J. J. Ryan
Lyons Katie, house Main near Morton

M

MACE JAMES, house Center District
Mack Perley A. farm hand, house Charles Shattuck
Madden John, Jr. house Center District
" Timothy, laborer, house Dean's block, Main
Maddox John, farmer, house river road, W. P.
" John, Jr. house Center District

Magowan Patrick, emp. Bradlee mill, house Oak, B. V.
Mahan Mary, house T. Dennie Thomson
Mahoney Mary, house Baker's lane
" John, laborer, house Mineral
" Patrick B. farmer, house river road, W. P.
Major Richard, coachman J. B. Smith, house Main
Malcolm Hugh, emp. Smith & Dove, house Lowell, W. P.
Malone Bridget Mrs. (Maurice) house Pearson
" Katherine E. emp. Tyer Rubber Co. h. Mrs. Bridget do.
" Margaret A. house Mrs. Bridget do.
Mander George, farmer, house Haverhill near High, F. V.
Manion Thomas H. house James O'Keefe

MANNING ALBERT S. (Smith & Manning) house Main near Locke
" John, house Baker's lane
Marinane Daniel, section hand B. & M. R. R. boards Patrick Donovan
" Dennis, section hand B. & M. R. R. boards Patrick Donovan
Marland Abraham, town clerk, house Chestnut near Central
" Charles H. station agent B. V. house Andover, B. V.
" Mary Mrs. (John) house 12 Brick block, A. V.
" Mary A. house Mrs. Mary do.
" Sarah Mrs. (William) house Chestnut c. Central

MARLAND WILLIAM, prop. Marland House, School near Main, house do.
Maroney John, house Center District
" John F. house Center District
" M. J. house Center District
" Patrick, emp. C. & K. house Andover, B. V.
Marsh Fannie, house Dr. Cecil F. P. Bancroft
Marshall James, clerk T. A. Holt & Co. house Maple av.
Marston Percival F. theological student, house Porter, P. D.

MASON CHARLES B. contractor and builder, house Abbot near Phillips
" L. E. Mrs. house High
" Sarah A. Mrs. (George F.) house off Main, S. D.
Maskell Nelson E. farm hand, house Pearson
Matthews Arthur T. foreman Bradlee mill, house Central, B. V.
" E. W. farmer, house High, F. V.
" John H. emp. C. & K. house Maple av. near Elm
" Thomas, overseer Bradlee mill, house Andover near railroad, B. V.
" William E. emp. C. & K. house Thomas do.
Matthison Olof, emp. C. & K. house Davis block, Centre, B. V.
May David M. emp. T. J. Farmer, house Mrs. Isabella W. do.

May Isabella W. Mrs. (Andrew) house Harding near railroad bridge
" James S. emp. J. S. Wakefield, h. Mrs. Isabella W. do.
Mayer Charles F. house Frye Village
" Samuel, milkman, house Samuel M. Jones
Mayers George A. harness maker, house High near Harding
" John, emp. Stevens mill, house Essex c. Baker's lane
McArdle Mary, domestic, house Maurice A. Roberts
McAvoy James, emp. Bradlee mill, house Oak, B. V.
McCallion Catherine Mrs. (William) h. North Main n. Marland
" John, emp. Stevens mill, house Marland, M. V.
McCarron Alice, house 7 Brick block, A. V.
" Mary A. house Alice do.
McCarthy Dennis A. house Timothy do.
" John, stone mason, house Pearson
" John, farmer, house Salem, H. D.
" John H. laborer, house North Main near the bridge
" Timothy, emp. Frank Gleason, house North Main near the bridge
McClellan Mary, house Margaret E. Gray
McClough Mary, house Edward P. Chapin
McCollum Francis, house John do.
" John, farmer, house off Lowell near J. W. Mooar, W. P.
" John, Jr. house John do.
" Rebecca, house Horace H. Tyer
" William, house John do.
McCombs Elizabeth, emp. Smith & Dove, bds. William Johnston
McCormick Michael, section foreman B. & M. R. R. house Essex c. Railroad
McCready Sarah Mrs. (Thomas) h. North Main n. river bridge
McCrorey James, emp. Smith & Dove, house Corbett, F. V.
McCullough Bridget Mrs. (John) house 12 Brook
" Isabel, dressmaker, house Mrs. Bridget do.
McCurdy Matthew S. Prof. instructor Phillips Academy, house Main opp. Chapel av.
McDermott Charles, flax dresser, house Baker's lane
" William H. house Charles do.
McDonald Christina, emp. Stevens mill, bds. Cornelius Sweeney
" Christine, domestic, house Miss Elizabeth Dow
" James, emp. Stevens mill, house Marland, M. V.
" John, emp. Smith & Dove, house Cuba
" John A. emp. Tyer Rubber Co. house foot School
McEnroe Linda Mrs. (Peter) house John P. Morgan
" Lizzie, house foot Sand, B. V.
McFarlane Katie, house Rev. John Phelps Taylor
McGlynn James, emp. Smith & Dove, house Baker's lane
" John, emp. Stevens mill, boards Patrick McNally

McGlynn William, emp. Stevens mill, boards Charles E. Torrey
McGovern Elizabeth Mrs. (Michael) house Tewksbury, B. V.
" Thomas, house Boston road, B. V.
" Thomas H. carpenter, house Tewksbury, B. V.
McGuinness John F. house Village District
" Margaret, house Charles A. Murphy
McGuire Ann, emp. Smith & Dove, boards Thomas W. Wilkie
McIntire Caroline Mrs. (Frederick) house Central near Main
" Daniel W. shoemaker, house off Main, S. D.
" John, emp. Bradlee mill, house Sand, B. V.
McIntosh David, emp. Marland mill, house High
" John, woolen dresser, house Pearson
" Mary Mrs. (James) house Essex, A. V.
McIsaac Maggie A. compositor, house Roderick do.
" Roderick, carpenter, house Florence
McKeen Philena, house Sunset Lodge, Abbot
McKenzie Alexander, machinist, house foot Essex
" Betsey, house 10 Brick block, A. V.
" Margaret, house 10 Brick block, A. V.
McKeon Grace Mrs. (James) house Sand, B. V.
McLaughlin Isabella Mrs. house Mineral, A. V.
McLAWLIN HENRY, hardware, paints, cordage, oils, etc., Main, house Elm opp. Florence
" Edith A. teacher, house Henry do.
McManus Mary Mrs. (Francis) house No. Main near Harding
McMellen Annie, domestic, house Mrs. Sarah Marland
McMillan Lizzie, domestic, house Miss Alice Rogers
McMullen Patrick, emp. Stevens mills, house Marland, M. V.
McNally Edward C. emp. Andover Steam Laundry, h. Thomas do.
" James R. spinner Stevens mill, house Thomas do.
" Joseph W. house Thomas do.
" John, emp. Stevens mill, boards Charles E. Torrey
" Patrick, emp. Stevens mill, house Marland, M. V.
" Thomas, house High c. Harding
McQueen William, baker, boards Robert Hodge
McTERNEN ANDREW, supt. Tyer Rubber Co. house Florence
" Maggie, emp. Tyer Rubber Co. boards John S. Harnden
" William H. foreman Tyer Rubber Co. house Harding near North Main
Meader Samuel, painter and paper hanger, house Porter
Mears Ada, house Mrs. Catherine do.
" Catherine Mrs. (Nathan) dressmaker, house Tewksbury, B. V.
" Calvin, emp. Bradlee mill, house Tewksbury, B. V.
" Charles, house near Lowell Junction station

Mears George W. policeman, house 13 Essex
" Nathan E. emp. Bradlee mill, house Centre, B. V.
" Warren, carpenter, house Oak, B. V.
Meldrum Frances W. teacher, house William A. do.
" John W. telegraph operater, house William A. do.
" William A. flax dresser, house Brook
Merrill Florence A. Mrs. (George C.) house 93 Main
" Lewis P. emp. Tyer Rubber Co. house High c. Harding
" Lucia G. teacher pianoforte, house Mrs. Lucia W. do.
" Lucia W. Mrs. (James H.) house Salem near Chapel av.
" Mary F. house Lewis P. do.
" Nelson A. carpenter, boards L. H. Eames
" Selah Rev. house Main
MESSER FRANK H. funeral director, Park, house Beard House, Elm
Metcalf ———, peddler, house Centre, B. V.
Middleton David, supt. Smith & Dove, house Haverhill, F. V.
" James, house Maple av.
" Margaret, house James do.
Midgley Elizabeth Mrs. confectionery, etc. house Mineral near the bridge, A. V.
Miller Edward A. student, house Charles H. Shaw
" Euphemia, house Main, F. V.
" Granville A. hairdresser 2 Pearson, house do.
" John, house Centre District
" Robert, teamster, house Marland, M. V.
" Thomas, emp. Bradlee mill, house River, B. V.
" William, boss weaver, house Sand, B. V.
" William, blacksmith, house Lowell, F. V.
Mills Frank S. house 49 Central
" Mary B. house 47 Central
" Rebecca B. Mrs. (Charles L.) house 49 Central
Millett Charles W. farm hand, house George D. do.
" Charles W. house Holt District
" George D. florist, house off Salem, H. D.
" George F. commercial salesman, h. Mrs. Martha M. do.
" Martha M. Mrs. (William P.) house Essex c. Brook
" Sidney S. bookkeeper, house Mrs. Martha M. do.
Milton Joseph, house Frye Village
Minkwitz Frederick, house Charles Fischer
Minor George S. house Elm near the square
Mitchell Annie D. variety store, Main, F. V. house do.
" Henry, florist, house off Salem, Jenkins' Corner, H. D.
Mooar J. Warren, carriage painter, Lowell, W. P. house do.
Moody Almon S. farmer, house Lowell, B. V.
" Clara E. teacher, house Almon S. do.
" Edwin C. farmer, house Almon S. do.

Moody Herbert A. carpenter and builder, house Lowell, B. V.
" Sarah M. nurse, house Almon S. do.
Mooney Philip, emp. Stevens mills, house No. Main n. Marland
Moore Charles A. student, house Prof. George F. do.
" C. H. Prof. instructor Phillips Academy, house Main opp. Chapel av.
" George F. Prof. professor in Theological Seminary, house Main near Chapel av.
Morgan John P. book agent, house Andover, B. V.
Moriarty John, emp. Bradlee mills, boards Mrs. Catherine Sherry
Morisy Isabella Mrs. house Maple av. near Elm
Moroney John, farmer, house Pearson
" John F. emp. C. & K. house John do.
" Kate, house John do.
" Michael J. laborer, house School c. Ridge
Morrill John A. house Center District
" May E. house Joseph H. do.
" Joseph H. house School c. Abbot
Morrison Agnes C. teacher, house Alexander do.
" Alexander, house Haverhill, F. V.
" Mary L. Mrs. house Andover, B. V.
" Nellie, house Andover, B. V.
" Rosella Mrs. house Poor, F. V.
Morse Catherine Mrs. (John C.) house John F. do.
" Charles, house Center District
" George A. emp. Tyer Rubber Co. house William B. do.
" George E. house Elm
" Gilbert, emp. Bradlee mill, house Sand, B. V.
" John F. carpenter, house Summer n. No. Andover line
" Leonard, house Osgood District
" William B. emp. Tyer Rubber Co. house Elm near High
" W. Byron, clerk H. McLawlin, house Maple av.
Morton Susan M. Mrs. (Rufus S.) house Main, S. D.
Moulton Charles N. house Osgood District
Mountain David I. house 8 Brick block, A. V.
Moynihan Jeremiah, emp. Stevens mills, house Marland, M. V.
" M. T. house Center District
Muise Theo, tailor, house Central near Main
Mulcahy James, house North District
Murch Llewellyn Capt. master mariner, house J. H. Batcheler place, B. V.
Murphy Charles A. house No. Main near railroad bridge
" Daniel, laborer, house W. P. District
" Daniel, Jr. emp. C. & K. house Daniel do.
" Dennis, emp. Stevens mill, house North Main n. Marland
" James, house North District
" John F. loom fixer, house North Main near Marland

Murphy John J. laborer, house Morton
" Patrick, house West Center District
" Thomas, bakery, ice cream, variety store, Main, house 1 Summer
Murray George E. (Murray Bros.) Lawrence, house Main near Lawrence line, F. V.
" Isabel, house Mrs. Maggie do.
" John W. emp. Bradlee mill, house Sand, B. V.
" Josephine, domestic, house Walter Buck
" Maggie Mrs. (John) house Sand, B. V.
" Mary A. domestic, house Walter Buck
" Walter, gardener, house Tewksbury, B. V.

MUSTER CHARLES M. carriage and sign painter, corner Park and Bartlet, house off Maple av.
Myers ——, house off Salem, H. D.
" Charles, (Myers & Son, harness makers) Barnard court, house Lowell, F. V.
" Ernest E. stone mason, house off Salem, H. D.
Myett Norman, house Morton
Myrascoff Eliza Mrs. emp. Smith & Dove, house Mineral.

N

NAPIER JAMES, house Center District
Nason Benjamin, carpenter, house Centre, B. V.
Neal O W. millinery, house Draper block, Main
" Horace S. emp. Bradlee mill, house foot Sand, B. V.
Nehr Herman F. supt. C. & K. house High, B. V.
Nelson Lindsay A. house North District
" William, house North District
Newcomb J. Edward, emp. Bradlee mill, house James E. do.
" James E. emp. Bradlee mill, house Andover, B. V.
Newhall Abbie S. Mrs. house Bancroft T. Haynes
Newman Charles H. photographer, house Henry J. do.
" Emma E. house Mrs. Martha M. Whitney
" Henry J. painter and grainer, house Bartlet opp. Punchard av.
" Margaret W. age 93 years, h. Mrs. Martha M. Whitney
" Samuel H. painter, boards Mrs. Louisa C. Roberts
Newton Charles H. farmer, house river road, W. P.
" W. R. instructor Phillips Academy, house 84 Main
Nice Henry, house Margaret M. E. Gray
" John, house Center District
Nichols J. Howard, house Ballard Vale
Nicholson Margaret, house Porter
Noessel Philip F. shipping clerk C. & K. house Chester, B. V.
Nolan Catherine Mrs. (Michael) house Highland road n. Salem

Nolan Ellen A. house Mrs. Ellen J. do.
" Ellen J. Mrs. (John) house North Main c. Pearson
" James, carpenter, house Cuba near Village
" Joseph P. tinsmith, house James do.
" Martin F. house Center District
" Mary T. emp. W. E. Rice, Lawrence, house James do.
Noyes Frank W. house Elm
" Frederick J. farmer, house near river road, W. P.
" Harriet Mrs. (Charles) house Elm near Walnut av.
" Harriet N. Mrs. house Central c. Brook
" Harry H. bookkeeper Tyer Rubber Co. house Elm near Walnut av.
" Henry P. furniture, Park, boards Mrs. Sarah E. Upton
" Willard, shoe mfr. house 41 Salem, P. D.
" Willard F. student, house Willard do.
Norris Nellie, dressmaker, Summer, boards Edwin Sulkoski
Northey Mary K. house 1 Chestnut
Nuckley John F. farmer, house off Main, S. D.
" Thomas F. house Scotland District
Nute Frank I. house High

O

O'Brien Dennis, farmer, house East Chestnut foot Carter's hill
" Ellen Mrs. (Dennis) house Pearson
" Honora Mrs. (Timothy) house Baker's lane
" Thomas J. stone mason, house Dennis do.
" Timothy, emp. H. P. Noyes, house Baker's lane
O'Connell Arthur F. carpenter, house East Chestnut
" David J. blacksmith, house Ridge off Brook
" John, wheelwright, Park, house Cuba
" John A. emp. Smith & Dove, house Lowell, W. P.
" Timothy, laborer, house Morton
" William, carpenter and builder, house Ridge
O'Connor David, blacksmith, house Ridge
" Nellie Mrs. house North Main near railroad bridge
" Michael J. stone mason, house Morton
" Patrick, shoemaker, house Blaney blk. Andover, B. V.
O'Connors Kate Mrs. boards Patrick McNally
Odlin Christianna Mrs. house Morton near Main
" William, counsellor-at-law, B. house Morton near Main
O'DONNELL HUGH, prop. Ballard Vale and Lawrence Express, Centre, B. V. house do.
" Hugh F. iron moulder, house Hugh do.
O'Hara Charles, farmer, house Village, W. P.
" Charles, farmer, house near J. W. Mooar's, W. P.
" Thomas, laborer, house W. P.

O'Hearn Ann Mrs. house Marland, M. V.
O'Keefe James, house Alms, F. V.
Oldroyd James, iron moulder, house Andover, B. V.
  " James, Jr. emp. Bradlee mill, house James do.
O'Leary Jeremiah, laborer, house foot Morton
  " John, carpenter, house Jeremiah do.
  " John, laborer, house foot Baker's lane
  " Mary E. house John do.
  " William H. laborer, house John do.
O'Neal John, emp. J. N. Smart, house do.
O'Neil Lucy, domestic, house Rev. Edwards A. Park
Osborne Frederick W. modeler, house Chester, B. V.
Ott Ernest, emp. C. & K. house Lowell, B. V.
Otis Margaret Mrs. (Charles P.) house Central corner Brook

P

PACKARD ALBION K. house George Graffam
Paine Katharine A. Mrs. (Edward S.) house Phillips
  " George, blacksmith, house Brook
Paine Joshua, house Center District
Palmer Frederic Rev. rector Christ church, house Central opp. Chestnut
  " William, gardener, house Alfred L. Ripley
  " William L. gardener, house Abbott
Paradis Mabel, house William T. do.
  " Charles W. house William T. do.
  " William T. house Porter corner Salem
Park Agnes, house Rev. Edwards A. do.
  " Edwards A. Rev. house Main opp. Chapel av.
Parker Charles S. house Summer
  " Converse F. fruit dealer, house William F. do.
  " Florence A. house Charles S. do.
  " George A. clerk Merrimack Mutual Fire Ins. Co. house Bartlet opp. intermediate school house
  " George H. druggist, Main, rooms Draper block, Main
  " George W. house River, B. V.
  " Mary C. forewoman C. & K. house William F. do.
  " William F. dealer in fruit and produce, house Marland, B. V.
Parkhurst Mary J. Mrs. house Tewksbury, B. V.
  " Frank E. clerk Dr. C. H. Shattuck, h. Mrs. Mary J. do.
Parton John, shoemaker, house Oak, B. V.
Partridge Lucy F. teacher, house George S. Minor
Pasho Bridget Mrs. house Baker's lane
  " Henry F. farmer, house Summer
  " James H. emp. Smith & Dove, house Mrs. Bridget do.

Patrick James S. overseer P. & C. Lawrence, house Poor, F. V.
Peabody Abbie H. house Main opp. Locke
" Ellen E. house Main opp. Locke
" Mary S. house Main opp. Locke
Pearson Charles H. teamster, house Andover, B. V.
" Edward B. commercial salesman, house Edward D. do.
" Edward D. emp. Bradlee mill, house Centre, B. V.
" Frank, farmer, house Main near South Main
" Fred, farmer, house Main near South Main
" George H. farmer, house Main n. South Main
" John, loom fixer, house North Main near Marland
" Joseph Mrs. house Main near South Main
" Walter B. emp. C. & K. house Edward D. do.
Pease Theodore C. Rev. prof. in Andover Theological Seminary, house Main c. Phillips
Pemberton Roland G. carpenter, house High
Penny Leander A. carpenter, house Marland, B. V.
Perham John F. carpenter, house Chester, B. V.
Perkins N. H. foreman B. F. Smith farm, house Phelps crossing, Haggett's pond
Perley Annie S. house Rev. John P. Gulliver
" Mary G. house Mrs. Lucia W. Merrill
Perry Charles J. wool sorter, house Sylvanus do.
" Nellie C. house Sylvanus do.
" Sylvanus, emp. Bradlee mill, house Lowell, B. V.
Pettee George D. teacher in Phillips Academy, house Bartlet c. Wheeler
Peters Joseph, house Frye Village
" Thomas, watchman Smith & Dove, boards Alfred G. Playdon
Phelps Dolly, house Phelps crossing, Haggett's pond
" Ella Mrs. (Sidney) house Anthony Ward
" Frank C. farmer, house near school house, W. P.
" Fred D. insurance, house Pearson
" Jane, house Salem, P. D.
" William H. house Morton near School
Phillips Alice, house Main c. Haverhill, F. V.
" Elizabeth, house Main c. Haverhill, F. V.
" Frank, machinist, house James F. do.
" James F. emp. Smith & Dove, house Union near Lawrence line, F. V.
" Samuel, house Woburn

PIDDINGTON GEORGE, florist, house School

" Jane, teacher, house George do.
Pierce Edith Mrs. house William S. Lawson

Pike Erwin C. stoves, tinware, plumbing, etc. Park, house Park c. Main
" George E. gardener, boards Elm House
Pillsbury George E. house Abbot District
" George P. farmer, house near Lowell, B. V.
Pitman Eugene, carpenter, house Elm
Platt Henry W. spinner, house Thomas W. do.
" Thomas W. carpenter, house Andover, B. V.
Playdon Alfred G. farmer and milk dealer, h. off Lowell, F. V.
" Calvert H. milkman, house Alfred G. do.

PLAYDON JOHN H. gardener and florist, house Alfred G. do.

Poland Austin S. carpenter, house Chestnut c. Main
" James, flax dresser, house foot Pearson
Pomeroy Henry L. watchman Tyer Rubber Co. house Mrs. Sarah A. do.
" Llewellyn D. emp. Tyer Rubber Co. house Mrs. Sarah A. do.
" Sarah A. Mrs. house 56 North Main near Harding
Poor Catherine, house Mrs. Catherine do.
" Catherine M. Mrs. (Jonathan) house Poor, F. V.
" Charles W. house 22 Essex
" Daniel H. wool sorter, house Mrs. Mary A. Fessenden

POOR GEORGE H. counsellor-at-law, B. house Main near Chestnut

POOR JOSEPH W. blacksmith, F. V. house Poor, F. V.

" Lincoln, bookkeeper Hide and Leather Nat. Bank, B. boards Joseph W. do.
" Mary M. house George H. do.
" Sara, house Mrs. Susan do.
" Susan Mrs. (James) house Punchard av. near Park

POOR WILLIAM, wagon manufacturer, Main, F. V. house do.

Porter John, emp. Smith & Dove, house Poor, F. V.
Pratt Thomas F. clerk, B. house Central near railroad bridge
Pray John, livery and boarding stable, Main, house do.
Pride Edward W. Rev. house 95 Main
Priest Sarah Mrs. (David) house Andover, B. V.
Price Edward, emp. C. & K. boards Edgar F. Sisco
" J. T. upholsterer, house Chester, B. V.
Purr James H. engineer at Draper Hall, house Abbot n. School
Putnam James N. farmer, house P. D. Smith farm, W. P.

Q

QUALEY JAMES E. emp. Stevens mill, house North Main
Quigley John F. spinner, house Marland, M. V.
Quimby Herbert, expressman, house Mrs. Mary do.
" Mary Mrs. house Punchard av. opp. Park
Quinn John, laborer, boards John J. Buckley
" Merter, house Center District
" Peter, house Center District
" William F. emp. C. & K. house River, B. V.

R

RALPH JOHN C. coachman, house Central
Ramsdell Harry A. bookkeeper, house Marshall L. do.
" Marshall L. house Main c. Chestnut
" Marshall L. Mrs. dry and fancy goods, Park, house 37 Main
Ramsden Henry, emp. Stevens mill, house North Main
Randall Esther Mrs. (Chandler P.) house Ira C. do.
" Ira C. agent R. G. Chase, nurseries, house Elm near Washington av.
" Susan E. Mrs. (Joel) house William Abbott
Rayner Elizabeth Mrs. house John Hilton
Rea Betsey, house Charles P. do.
" Charles P. teaming and jobbing, house Park n. Florence
" Grace, dressmaker, house Charles P. do.
" Jasper, farmer, house Elm near Washington av.
" William T. house Center District
Ready Mary, house Sylvanus Perry
Reed Charles, house West District
" Edwin, house School opp. Abbot Academy
" Ellen, boards Charles E. Torrey
" Mary A. Mrs. house Richard C. do.
" Richard C. carpenter, house Prospect near Prospect hill
" William J. painter, house Elm near the square
" William M. astronomer at Harvard Observatory, house Edwin do.
Regan Margaret Mrs. (John) house Pearson
" William P. architect, house Pearson
Reidy Margaret Mrs. house Oak, B. V.
Remington Augustus, emp. Tyer Rubber Co. boards Darius Richardson
Renwick Mary Mrs. domestic, house William Shaw
Reynolds James H. house Frye Village
Rhodes Thomas, house North Main

RHODES THOMAS E. prop. Electric Car Station and teacher piano-forte, house 19 North Main
" E. Alice, dressmaker, house Thomas E. do.
" Walter, clerk Thomas E. Rhodes, house North Main
Richard Fred, emp. C. & K. house Blaney block, Andover, B. V.
Richards James F., M. D. physician and surgeon, house Main c. Punchard av.
" Mary A. Mrs. bookkeeper W. F. Draper, rooms Draper block, Main
" Susan B. Mrs. (John) house Chestnut
Richardson Abbie A. house Main c. Morton
" A. Clark, carpenter and builder, house Maple av.
" Ammon P. house West District
" Darius, house East Chestnut
" Ellen P. house Samuel S. do.
" J. H. prop. Thorndale stock farm, off Elm near North Andover line, house do.
" John W. carpenter, house Elm near Washington av.
" Samuel S. house 35 Salem, P. D.
" H. Maria, house Main c. Morton
" Wesley, laborer, house off Maple av.
Riebe Henry M. machinist, house Tewksbury, B. V.
" William F. machinist, house Henry M. do.
Riley B. Henry, house John do.
" James, house Ballard Vale
" James Mrs. house River, B. V.
" John, emp. Smith & Dove, house 6 Brick block, A. V.
" John, spinner, house River, B. V.
" John, Jr. bookkeeper C. & K. house John do.
" John A. emp. Bradlee mill, house Patrick do.
" Lawrence F. emp. Bradlee mill, house High, B. V.
" Michael H. emp. C. & K. boards Mrs. Richard J. Sherry
" Patrick, emp. Bradlee mill, house River, B. V.
" Peter, laborer, house Lowell road, O. D.
" Terence, emp. Bradlee mill, boards Mrs. Richard J. Sherry
Ring Henry W. emp. Tyer Rubber Co. boards James A. Holt
Ripley Alfred L. vice-president Nat. Hide and Leather Bank, Boston, house Central near School
" George, house Central
" George B. house Alfred L. do.
" Mary, house Alfred L. do.
Roach Michael, farmer, house East Chestnut n. Highland road
Robb Margaret Mrs. (Charles) house Haverhill n. railroad bridge, F. V.
Roberts Louisa C. Mrs. (James P.) house Bartlet near Park
" Mary K. house Abbot c. Phillips

Roberts Morris A. salesman, B. house School near Main
Robertson David, emp. C. & K. house Peter do.
" Peter, foreman Smith & Dove, house Village near Cuba
Robinson Elmer E. house Abbot District
" Henry S. Atlantic Works, B. h. Punchard av. n. Main
" Joseph T. emp. Smith & Dove, house Union near Lawrence line, F. V.
" Joseph T. Jr. emp. Brainard Cummings, h. Joseph T. do.
" Thomas, hostler, boards Elm House
" William C. blacksmith, house Joseph T. do.
" William E. farmer, house Union n. Lawrence line, F. V.
" William H. boss dresser, house North Main near Simpson's bridge
Roger George, emp. Smith & Dove, house Essex c. Baker's lane
Rogers Alice, house Main c. Morton
" Barnett, real estate and insurance, office Main c. Essex, house High near Harding
" John, boards Mrs. Bessie R. Hill
Ronan Catherine Mrs. (William) house Morton
" John J. carpenter, house Morton
" John S. emp. George Chandler, house Morton
" William S. painter, house Mrs. Catherine do.
Rooney Mary A. domestic, house Miss Ella T. Cheever
Ropes James H. house Bartlet
" Joseph, farmer, house George F. Baker
" William L. Rev. librarian in Andover Theological Seminary, house Bartlet
Rose M. Agnes, house Mrs. Elizabeth L. Abbott
Ross Ralph R. mason, house William R. do.
" William R. mason, house Centre, B. V.

ROWE E. J. paper hanger and decorator, house Phillips

Rowland Lizzie M. house Joseph Shaw
" Sleigh, house Sand, B. V.
Russell Agnes, house Joseph W. Smith
" Henry A. carpenter, house 8 Summer
" J. laborer, house Centre, B. V.
" John G. emp. A. B. Bruce, Lawrence, h. Lowell, F. V.
" Mary Mrs. (Winslow) house Thomas W. Platt
" Martha A. Mrs. (George) house near the church, W. P.
" Moody, house Summer
Ryan Ellen, house Rev. J. J. Ryan
" Rev. J. J. pastor St. Augustine's church, h. 30 Essex
Ryder William H. Rev. prof. in Theological Seminary, house 89 Main

S

SADLIER THOMAS, house Ballard Vale
" William F. buffer C. & K. house River, B. V.
Salgstrom Ellen, domestic, house Edwin Reed
Salmon Mary Mrs. (David) house Andover, B. V.
Sampson Frederick A. farmer, house Corbett, F. V.
" George R. house 25 Salem
Sanborn C. H. A. Miss, teacher of pianoforte, house Morton near School
" E. M. E., M. D., Miss, physician, house Morton n. School
" M. E. P., Miss, dressmaker, house 73 Main
Sandford Charles, emp. Alfred L. Ripley, house do.
" Charles A. house foot Abbot
" George M. house High near Elm square
Sargent Ruth Mrs. (Thomas H.) house Marland, B. V.
Saunders Ann Mrs. (James) house Cuba
" Antoine B. clerk Hide and Leather Bank, B. h. John do.
" George, stoves, ranges, etc. Main, house High n. Harding
" Harry W. house James M. do.
" James M. farmer, house off Maple av.
" John, supt. Smith & Dove, house Essex c. Railroad
" Warren, farmer, house river road, W. P.
Sawyer Fannie, house Miss Elizabeth Dow
" Sarah L. house Prospect near Prospect hill
Scammon A. Leland, Miss, vocal culture, h. Miss Margaret S. Jarvie
" J. Quincy, house Abbot near Phillips
Schneider Louis H. iron moulder, house Tewksbury, B. V.
Schofield John, watchman C. & K. house Cuba
" Samuel, carpenter, house Marland, M. V.
Schwartz Charles, emp. C. & K. house Marland, B. V.

SCOTT C. W., M. D., physician and surgeon, office and residence Main near Punchard av., office hours 1 to 3 and 7 to 9 p. m.

" Edward, foreman card room Bradlee mill, h. Andover, B. V.
" James, gardener, house Mineral

Scott James F. house Ballard Vale
" John W. foreman Bradlee mill, house Edward D.
" Margaret, house James do.
" Margaret W. emp. Smith & Dove, house James do.
" Patrick J. wool sorter Bradlee mill, house Andover, B.V.
" Sadie C. house Theodore C. Georgi
" William, emp. office Andover Townsman, house James do.
Seacole Henry, emp. Stevens mill, house Marland, M. V.

SEARS JOHN C. boots, shoes and rubbers, house 52 Punchard av.
" Sarah E. house John C. do.
Sellers Arthur W. L. foreman Lawrence American, house William T. do.
" William T. editor Lawrence Evening Tribune, house Poor, F. V.
Sewell Asa O. house High
Shannon Daniel F. house Summer c. Punchard av.
Shapleigh William P. carpenter, boards Mrs. Louisa C. Roberts
Shattuck Arthur M. emp. C. & K. house Nathan H. do.
" Caroline A. Mrs. florist, house off South Main, S. D.
" Charles, farmer, house Lowell, W. P.
" Charles H. harness maker, Main, house Punchard av. rear Punchard school house

SHATTUCK CHARLES H., M. D. physician and surgeon, office Drug Store, Ballard Vale, residence do.

" Elmer H. constable, house Nathan H. do.
" Frederick H. milk dealer, house off South Main, S. D.
" Minnie A. house Charles H. do.
" Nathan H. harness maker, house off Punchard av. rear Punchard school house
" Nathan H. gate tender C. & K. house Chester, B. V.
" Sarah, house Lowell, W. P.
" Sarah E. (Brown & Shattuck) house Bartlet
" Scott T. hack driver, house Charles H. do.
Shaw Arthur J. painter and paper hanger, house Marland block, Centre, B. V.
" Benjamin, spinner, house Centre, B. V.
" Charles H. operative Bradlee mill, house foot Centre, B.V.

Shaw David, house East Chestnut near Punchard av.
" George, house Centre, B. V.
" Henry, painter and paper hanger, house Marland block, Centre, B. V.
" John B. painter and paper hanger, house Tewksbury road, O. D.
" Joseph, superintendent Ballard mill, house Andover, B.V.
" Stephen R. house Village, A. V.
" William, pub. agent Christian Society, house Tewksbury, B. V.
" William, house Osgood District
Shea Annie Mrs. (Patrick) house Salem, H. D.
" Ellen Mrs. (Bartholomew) house Porter
" Michael O. house Morton near Main
Shearer Charles H. house Mrs. Mary L. do.
" Mary L. Mrs. house Abbott
Sheehan Daniel, emp. Frank Gleason, house Pearson
Sheldon Luther H. Rev. house Main near Porter
Sherman Minnie Mrs. house Summer near Punchard av.
Sherry Catherine Mrs. (James) house Blaney blk. Andover, B. V.
" James, plater C. & K. boards Mrs. Richard J. Sherry
" Joseph T. emp. Bradlee mill, house Andover, B. V.
SHERRY RICHARD J. meat and provisions, Tewksbury, B. V. house Tewksbury corner Andover, do.
" Richard J. Mrs. boarding house, house Tewksbury corner Andover, B. V.
Shevlin Peter, farmer, house Porter, P. D.
Shirrell Sarah L. Mrs. (William) house Mrs. Abbie H. Abbott
Shore James, emp. Stevens mill, boards Mrs. Mary Lord
Shute George E. house Osgood District
Simons Fred, farmer, house Salem near Prospect Hill
" Fred, Jr. teaming and jobbing, house Salem n. Prospect hill, H. D.
" Henry W. laborer, house Highland road near Salem
" Richard W. house North District
Simpson Allan, second hand Bradlee mill, house Sand, B. V.
" George, dresser tender Bradlee mill, house Andover near railroad, B. V.
Sinclair Gertrude E. house James E. Dennison
Sisco Edgar F. emp. C. & K. house Tewksbury, B. V.
Skene Agnes, house Mineral
" George A. gardener P. D. Smith, house Village
Sleath William H. foreman C. & K. house Centre, B. V.
Smart James N. house off Main near South Main
" James N. printer B. house Gardner av. P. D.
" Joseph A. secretary and treasurer Merrimack Mutual Fire Ins. Co. Bank building, house Main

Smith Ann, Mrs. house Mrs. Ann Higginbottom
" Benjamin F. house 48 Central
" Benjamin F. house Phelps crossing, Haggett's pond
" Bridget Mrs. (James) house Oak, B. V.
" Carrie E. Mrs. (G. Emory) house Joseph Abbott
" Charles F. emp. A. W. W. house John L. do.
" Edward, house West District
" Elizabeth Mrs. (George) house Poor, F. V.
" Frank M. emp. A. fire dept. house Elm
" Fred, painter, rooms William J. Reed
" George, brass spinner C. & K. boards Mrs. Richard J. Sherry
" George A. house Joseph Abbott
" George F. house Joseph W. do.
" James, emp. Smith & Dove, house Haverhill, F. V.
" James B. president Smith & Dove Mfg. Co. house Main
" James L. clerk, house Main
" John E. superintendent water works, house High near Harding
SMITH JOHN L. (Smith & Manning) groceries, dry goods, etc. Essex, house High
" Joseph W. (Smith & Dove) house Main, F. V.
" Julia A. Mrs. (George) house High near Elm square
" Laura F. Mrs. (Thomas) house Post-office av.
" Peter D. house Village corner Marland
" Walter L. plumber, house Summer near Punchard av.
" William C. farm hand, house Daniel Harrington
" William D. house Joseph W. do.
Smithson Jane A. Mrs. house North Main near Simpson's bridge
Smyth Prof. Egbert C. prof. Theological Seminary, house Main near Salem
Soehrens John H. hairdresser, Main, house Punchard av. n. Park
Soutar James, 2d, emp. Smith & Dove, house Main c. Haverhill, F. V.
" James, emp. Smith & Dove, house Mineral, A. V.
" Joseph M. house Village
" Walter W. house Abbot District
Spark William, emp. Smith & Dove, house Haverhill, F. V.
Spaulding Jonas, manufacturer, house Bartlet near Morton
Speckler George, house Osgood District
Spence James, clerk Merrimack Mutual Fire Ins. Co. house High near Harding
" Laura A. house James do.
Spencer Rebecca, boards Mrs. Ruth Sargent
" Kate, boards Mrs. Ruth Sargent
Stack John, house Pearson
" John, Jr. sexton St. Augustine church, house Pearson

Stack Michael, teaming and jobbing, house Pearson
Stapleton Margaret, domestic, house Prof. Matthew S. McCurdy
Starbuck Charles C. Rev. house 23 Salem
Stark John S. meat and provisions, house Marland, B. V.
" John W. clerk, house John S. do.
" William D. house Tewksbury, B. V.
Stearns William, house Center District
Steele Katherine, house Mrs. Maria Suart
Steffens Christopher, emp. C. & K. house George W. do.
" George W. emp. C. & K. house Andover, B. V.
Stephen David, emp. Tyer Rubber Co. house Village, A. V.
Sterling John S. emp. Smith & Dove, boards Mrs. Ann Higginbottom
Stevens A. J. Mrs. house Mrs. Mary A. Underwood
" Enoch O. house North District
Stewart Bessie, domestic, house Edward B. Hutchinson
" George, house Pearson
" James, flax sorter, house Cuba
" John, watchman O. C. depot, house Pearson
" John, hairdresser, Chapman block, house North Main
" John W. house Mrs. Polly A. do.
" Polly A. Mrs. house North Main
STICKNEY CHARLES C. (Stickney & Howell) carpenter and builder, house Boston road, B. V.
" Charles O. boards Miss Nellie E. Morrison
Stiles Carrie T. house Mrs. Lydia E. Adams
" George W. carpenter, house Washington av. n. Summer
Stinson Fred, house Phillips District
Stone Charles E. instructor Phillips Academy, house 59 Main
" Colver J. student, house Charles H. Gilbert
" James, house George P. Pillsbury
" Charles N. L. milkman, house High. F. V.
Stork W. Boteler, student, house Nathan Ellis
" Maria H. Mrs. (Rev. Charles A.) house Nathan Ellis
Stott A. Sewall, painter, house Union near Lawrence line, F. V.
" George L. tinsmith, house Union n. Lawrence line, F. V.
" Joshua H. carpenter, house Union junc. Main, F. V.
" Thomas E. wool sorter, house River, B. V.
Stover George W. farmer, house off Salem, H. D., near N. A. line
Stritch John, emp. Bradlee mill, house foot Sand, B. V.
Sturoc Margaret, house Lowell, F. V.
Suart Maria Mrs. house High
Sulkoski Edwin, emp. Tyer Rubber Co. house Summer c. Elm
Sullivan Cornelius, bookkeeper, boards John do.
" Daniel, mason, house Morton
" Jeremiah, house Poor, F. V.
" John, emp. Smith & Dove, house Owen do.

Sullivan John, laborer, house North Main near railroad bridge
" Michael F. house Daniel do.
" Owen, ink maker, house Corbett, F. V.
" Owen, emp. Stevens mill, house Alms, F. V.
" Owen, Jr. emp. Donald Ink Works, house Owen do.
" Patrick, emp. Smith & Dove, house Owen do.
" Patrick, house West Center District
" Patrick, emp. Smith & Dove, house Poor, F. V.
" Timothy C. house West Center District
Sutcliffe Frederick, foreman Stevens mill, house Summer corner Punchard av.
Swallow Frederick A. emp. Stevens mill, boards David C. Eastwood
Swanton Cora I. house Samuel A. do.
" Frederick A. farmer, house Samuel A. do.
" Samuel A. painter, house 60 Salem, H. D.
Sweeney Cornelius, section hand B. & M. R. R. house No. Main near railroad bridge
" Daniel, emp. Tyer Rubber Co. house Dennis do.
" Daniel, laborer, house John do.
" Dennis, farmer, house off Salem, H. D.
" Dennis, blacksmith and wheelwright Pearson cor. Main, house off Salem, H. D.
" Dennis, 2d, blacksmith Pearson, house John do.
" John, farmer, house off Salem, H. D.
" John, carpenter, house Roger do.
" John C. butcher, house John do.
" Roger, emp. Smith & Dove, house North Main near railroad bridge
Swift Almena J. Mrs. (Jonathan) house Central c. Brook
" Charlotte, house George F. do.
" George F. house Main c. Chestnut
" Kate A. house Mrs. Almena J. do.
" Martha E. house George F. do.
Symonds Flint A. laborer, house Washington av. near Summer
" Henry W. emp. Fred M. Hill, house Highland road off Salem

T

Tarbox John, boards Central Street Dining Room
Tardiff George, carpenter, house Ridge
Taylor Abel W. laborer, house Marland block, Centre, B. V.
" George F. emp. Stevens mill, house North Main near Marland
" John Phelps Rev. prof. Biblical History, house 38 School
" Margaret Mrs. house Main, F. V. near Lawrence line

Taylor Radcliffe, boards Abel W. do.
" Thomas, emp. Stevens mill, house No. Main
Teague Elwyn, emp. Bradlee mill, house foot Sand, B. V.
Terrill William H. house Phillips District
Thayer Samuel, farmer, house Prospect near Prospect Hill
Thomes Samuel, carpenter, house 8 Washington av.
" William C. carpenter, house Samuel do.
Thompson Andrew, painter, house Cuba corner Mineral
" John H. carpenter, house East Chestnut
Thomson T. Dennie, (Thomson & Fessenden) linen importer B. house 41 Central
Thwing Charles W. clerk J. S. Stark, house Marland, B. V.
Tilton Mary B. house Mrs. Rebecca A. do.
" Rebecca A. Mrs. house Salem near Chapel av.
Timlin —— Mrs. house Salem, P. D.
Tobey Mary A. Mrs. (Samuel L.) house Salem c. Porter
Tobin Kate Mrs. (John) house Blaney block, Andover, B. V.
" Mary, domestic, house James P. Butterfield
Torr George H. treas. Smith & Dove Co. h. Phillips c. Central
Torrey Charles E. boarding house, Marland, M. V. house do.
" John P. house Center District
Tough Alvin, house John do.
" John W. gate tender B. & M. R. R. house Summer opp. Washington av.
Towle Anna M. house Jonathan do.
" Jonathan, house 73 Main
" N. C. Dr. house Rev. Frederic Palmer
Towne Joseph H. Rev. house 36 Salem, P. D.
" Kate W. house Rev. Joseph H. do.
" Mary W. house Punchard av. near Park
Townley William, house Bailey District
Townsend Charlotte, domestic, house Rev. Frederick W. Greene
Toye James, house North District
Tracy William, emp. S M. Downs, house Chestnut corner Main
Trahan John, house 5 Village
" Sarah, house Ezra H. Valpey
Trautmann William, emp. C. & K. house Centre, B. V.
Trefry Edward E. clerk J. H. Campion, house Elm r. Elm House
Trow Daniel L. farmer, house Lowell, W. P.
" Ida M. Mrs. (George) house Daniel L. do.
" William A. house Daniel L. do.
Troy Michael, soap maker, house Pearson
Trulan John H. emp. Stevens mill, house Mrs. Mary do.
" Mamie E. house Mrs. Mary do.
" Mary Mrs. (William) house Essex, A. V.

TRULAN WILLIAM F. variety store, Essex, A. V. house Mrs. Mary do.

Tschauder Joseph, farmer, house Andover, B. V. r. H. A. Beeley's
" Joseph, Jr. house Joseph do.
Tuck Hannah A. Mrs. (John) house Lowell, W. P.
" M. Warren, house Lowell, W. P.
Tucker E. H. Mrs. house William H. Tucker
" William H. farmer, house off Salem, H. D. n. N. A. line
" William J. house Phillips District
Tulley Thomas, emp. J. H. Campion, rooms Edward Trefry
Turner Mary B. emp. Bradlee mill, house Patrick do.
" Patrick, emp. Bradlee mill, house foot Sand, B. V.
TUTTLE BENJAMIN B. prop. Brown's Express, Park, house Elm
" Howard, carpenter, boards George E. Murray
Twichell Jane W. Mrs. (Edward) house Mrs. Mary D. Hall
" Julia E. house Mrs. Mary D. Hall
TYER HORACE H. president Tyer Rubber Co. house Chestnut corner Central
Tyler Charles F. house Centre District
" Nancy M. Mrs. (Eben D.) house Bartlet near Chestnut

U

UNDERWOOD MARY A. MRS. house Main junc. Porter
Upton Augustus, farmer, house Osgood District
" Benjamin F. emp. Tyer Rubber Co. boards 8 Summer
" Lucy J. Mrs. (John A.) house Kimball House, Elm
" Sarah E. (Lysander E.) house East Chestnut

V

VALENTINE FRANK, house West District
VALPEY EZRA H. (Valpey Bros.) house 12 Summer

Van Vleck B. H. asst. at Boston Society of Natural History, house Abbott
Vennard Oliver W. sexton Old South church, house Central near Phillips

W

WAGNER WILLIAM E. laborer, house Maple av. near Elm
Wagstaff Sarah Mrs. (John) house Lowell, W. P.
WAKEFIELD JOHN P. meat and provisions, Main c. Park, house Cuba
Wakeley William, emp. Bradlee mill, house Andover, B. V.
Waldo Joseph W. carpenter, house Miss Mary do.
" Mary, house off Main, S. D.

Waldo Roxanna Mrs. (Jonathan) house Main, S. D.
Walker B. S. house Bailey District
" Caroline Mrs. house Chester, B. V.
" Isabella, house 50 Central
" Martin, laborer, boards John J. Adams
" Martin L. house Mrs. Caroline do.
" Winslow, carpenter, house Center District
Walls Pascal, farmer and poultry fancier, house off Salem, Jenkius' Corner, North Reading line, H. D.

WALSH MICHAEL T. stoves, tinware, plumbing, etc. Essex, house do.

Wanamaker Millard C. baggage master Lowell Junc. boards H. J. Gardner
Warburton Abraham, machinist, house No. Main near railroad bridge
Warcup Jane, domestic, house Henry S. Robinson
Ward Anthony, farmer, house Lowell, F. V.
" Emma L. teacher, house Anthony do.
" George D. farmer, house Lowell, F. V.
" Maggie, house Anthony do.
" Mary E. Mrs. in summer house Main near Lawrence line, F. V.
" Peter, fireman, house Ballard Vale road, B. V.
" Richard A. milk dealer, house Lowell, F. V.
" Samuel, emp. Tyer Rubber Co. house Center District
" Wilbur F. overseer Bradlee mill, house foot Sand
Warden Christina Mrs. (Charles) house William do.
" William, house foot School
Wardman Jabez, farmer, house Tewksbury road, O. D.
Wardwell Benjamin F. house Summer c. Washington av.
" Herbert, house Bailey District
" Joseph W. livery and boarding stable, house Lowell Junction, Andover, B. V.
Waterman Fred, laborer, house off Morton near Main
Watson Helen, emp. Tyer Rubber Co. house James do.
" James, house High
" Jessie Mrs. house Main junc. Porter
" Robert A. farmer, house Isaac Carruth
Webb David, house Bailey District
" Reuben, house Bailey District
Webster Nathan, farmer, house river road, W. P.
" Stephen, house North District
Weeks John, carpenter, house Florence
Welch Ann Mrs. house Morton
" Ellen E. house Michael do.
" Michael T. mason, house North Main near Marland
" Patrick, shoemaker, h. East Chestnut foot Carter's hill

Weld Arthur B. house Phillips District
" Fred M. emp. C. & K. house Mrs. Maria do.
" Maria Mrs. (Marcellus) house Porter, P. D.
Wenzel Otto, house Centre, B. V.
West Howard, house Osgood District
Whipple Frances A. Mrs. house East Chestnut near Main
Whitcomb David, house Center District
White Edward, emp. Stevens mill, house Marland, M. V.
" Frank D. house Center District
" Frank O. job printer, house Mrs. Mary S. do.
" Otis, farmer, house Boston road, B. V.
" Mary A. house William do.
" Mary S. Mrs. (Burnham S.) house High near Harding

WHITE MOORS E. mason and contractor, office Essex, house do.
" Roswell B. carpenter, house Punchard av. opp. Park
" Thomas, house West Center District
" William, laborer, house No. Main near railroad bridge
" William W. carpenter, boards Roswell B. do.

WHITING JOHN E. watchmaker and jeweler Barnard block, house Maple av.

Whitman David, foreman Thorndale stock farm, house do.
Whitney E. A. Mrs. dressmaker, house Bartlet cor. Morton
" Martha M. Mrs. (Charles A.) house 44 Salem, P. D.
Whittaker Henry S. machine printer, house Charles H. Johnson
" Lawrence, house Tewksbury, B. V.
Whittemore Grace M. Mrs. (Frederick W.) house 86 Main
" Abbie M. Mrs. (Charles P.) house Mrs. Katharine A. Paine
Whittier Edwin H. house Centre, B. V.
Wiggin Albert B. house Main opp. Salem
" George W. prop. Central Street Dining Room, house do.
" James L. cook Central Street Dining Room, house George W. do.
" Frances S. house Albert B. do.
Wilbur Arthur S. house Center District
" Fred C. conductor L. L. & H. R. R. house Maple av. c. Walnut av.
" Henry R. Rev. house High
" Melville R. carpenter, boards George Cummings
" Susy M. principal Central Grammar school, house Rev. Henry R. do.
Wilde William E. house North District
Wildes Mary T. Mrs. (George T.) house School corner Locke
Wiley Mary A. Mrs. (William) house Bartlet corner Morton
Wilkie Thomas W. emp. Smith & Dove, house Village, A. V.
Wilkins Luna A. student, house E. C. Pike

Williams H. D. house Center District
Williamson Francis J. plasterer, house Mrs. Margaret do.
" Margaret Mrs. (Francis) house near foot Morton
" Richard, stone mason, house W. P. District
Willey Alexander, emp. Smith & Dove, house Essex cor. Baker's lane
Winning Alexander Mrs. house Daniel Harrington
Winters Michael, emp. Stevens mill, house Marland, M. V.
Winton David J. painter and paper hanger, house Centre, B. V.
" Jane Mrs. (Matthew) house Centre, B. V.
" Thomas W. painter, house Centre, B. V.
Wilson Alexander, house Haverhill near railroad bridge, F. V.
" Frederick A. Rev. pastor of the Free Christian church, house Railroad near the church
" Howell F. paymaster Ballard Vale mills, house Andover, B. V.
" William, house Center District
Winn Fred E. house Phillips District
Withum John B. shoe mfr. house off Main, S. D. in summer
Wollfenden John, emp. Stevens mill, house Harding c. No. Main
Wombwell Charles, foreman C. & K. house Centre, B. V.
Wood Eden Mrs. (James) house Chester, B. V.
" James, spinner, house Mrs. Eden do.
" John H. spinner Bradlee mill, house foot Sand, B. V.
" Newell, printer, house George H. Burnham
" William, painter and paper hanger Park, house Florence
" William M. general manager Washington mills, Lawrence, house Main, F. V.
" William W. house William do.
Woodbridge Anna M. Mrs. (Benjamin F.) house Highland road, Carter hill
" Charles, shoemaker, house off Salem, Jenkins corner, H. D.
" Perley F. cider manufacturer, house Salem, H. D.

WOODLIN ABBIE A. MRS. (Greene & Woodlin) house Centre, B. V.

Woods Elizabeth A. house Bartlet corner Wheeler
Woodwell C. S. Mrs. house Morton corner Main
Woodworth Mary A. Mrs. house Daniel F. Shannon
Worthley Phebe M. house Bartlet near Chestnut
Wright Edgar G. farmer, house off Lowell, W. P.
" Harland P. boots, shoes and rubbers, Barnard's block Main, house Elm
" Harry S. tinsmith, house off Mineral, W. C. D.
" Herbert, house Harland P. do.
" Thomas, emp. Lawrence mill, house Boston road, B. V.
" William, house Ballard Vale
Wrigley Ann Mrs. (William) house Thomas E. Rhodes

Wrigley Simeon, spinner, house North Main n. Simpson's bridge
" Thomas, emp. Stevens mill, house North Main near Simpson's bridge
Wyllie Alexander, house Frye Village

Y

York Richard, emp. C. & K. house Oak, B. V.
" Leonard, emp. C. & K. house Richard
Young A. D. house West District
" John C. emp. Smith & Dove, boards Mrs. Ann Higginbottom
" Levi C. painter and paper hanger, house Highland road, Carter's hill
Youngson Jeannette Mrs. (David) house Lowell, F. V.

Z

Zang Emma, domestic, house George H. Torr
Zetterman Albert, emp. William M. Wood, bds. Carl Lindquist

"The only advertising medium for Andover."

✤ THE ✤
ANDOVER TOWNSMAN.

JOHN N. COLE,   GEORGE A. HIGGINS,
Managing Editor.   Local Editor.

ANDOVER, MASS.

The Townsman is the only newspaper published in Andover. It has five times the local circulation of all other newspapers dealing with Andover news. Always alive and progressive, placing foremost Andover's progress and best welfare.

PUBLISHED BY

THE ANDOVER PRESS,
The LEADING PRINTERS of ESSEX COUNTY.

JOHN N. COLE, Treasurer and Manager.

VALPEY BROTHERS,
(Established 1866,)
———DEALERS IN———
Meats, : Vegetables, : Poultry,
ETC., ETC.

No. I MAIN STREET, cor. ELM SQUARE,
Andover.

G. H. VALPEY.   E. H. VALPEY.

Andover Business Directory.

Agricultural Implements.

McLAWLIN HENRY, Main (see inside last cover)

Artist.

GEORGI THEODORE C. Washington av. (see page 3)

Attorneys and Counsellors-at-Law.

FOSTER GEORGE W. office Bank bldg. Main (see page 47)
Poor George H. office Carter block, Main

Auctioneers.

Cole George S. Chestnut
Rogers Barnett, office Main c. Essex

Band.

Andover Brass Band, Arthur Bliss, leader

Bakers.

Andover Bakery, Park
KEELAND J. E. Andover, B. V. (dealer) (see page 2)
Murphy Thomas, Main

Banks.

ANDOVER NATIONAL BANK, Moses Foster cashier (see page 8)
Andover Savings Bank, John F. Kimball treasurer and clerk

Bicycle Agent.

CHASE HERBERT F. Post Office av. (see page 16)

Billiard and Pool Rooms.

ELM HOUSE (see page 18)
Ledwell William T. Park

Blacksmiths.

ANDERSON & BOWMAN, Park c. Bartlet (see adv. index)
HARRIMAN THOMAS P. Park (see page 4)
POOR WILLIAM, Main, F. V. (see page 26)
Sweeney Dennis, Pearson c. Main

Boarding Houses.

Eastman Ira A. Porter (students of Phillips Academy)
Ellis Nathan, Main c. Morton (students of Phillips Academy)
MARLAND HOUSE, School (students of Phillips Academy) (see page 11)
Sherry Richard J. Mrs. Tewksbury, B. V.
Torrey Charles E. Marland, M. V.

Booksellers and Stationers.

ANDOVER BOOK STORE, Main, J. N. Cole (see page 86)
Chandler John H. Main
JOYCE P. V. Tewksbury, B. V. (see page 2)

Boots, Shoes and Rubbers.

Brown Benjamin, Main
DALY P. J. Elm square (see red page C)
GREENE & WOODLIN, Andover, B. V. (see over adv. ind.)
SEARS JOHN C. Bank building, Main (see last cover)
Wright Harlan P. Main

Boot and Shoe Makers and Repairers.

Ashworth James, Andover, B. V.
Brown Benjamin, Main
Chase Wallace N. Andover, B. V.
Craik James, Mineral, A. V.
Gibbs Theodore A. Oak, B. V.

Boot and Shoe Mfrs.

Barnard Henry W. Post Office av.
Jaquith Newton, Main, S. D.

Box Mfrs.

Hardy & Cole, Essex
Ladd H. P. Ballard Vale

Carpenters and Builders.

CUMMINGS BRAINARD, Park c. Bartlet (see inside last cover)
Hardy & Cole, Essex
MASON C. B. Old Abbott Store bldg. Main (see red page B)
O'Connell William, Ridge
STICKNEY & HOWELL, Summer (see page 8)

Carriage Mfrs.

POOR WILLIAM, Main, F. V. (see page 26)

Carriage Painters.

Mooar J. Warren, Lowell, W. P.
MUSTER CHARLES M. Park (see page 26)
POOR WILLIAM, Main, F. V. (see page 26)

Carpets, Oil Cloths, Etc.

Noyes H. P. Park
SMITH & MANNING, Essex (see page 28)

Caterers.

Wiggin George W. Central

Cigars, Tobacco, Etc.

[See also Druggists and Grocers.]

Bacigalupo L. J. & Co. Main
Clinton John H. off Andover, B. V.
ELM HOUSE, Elm square (see page 18)
JOYCE PATRICK V. Tewksbury, B. V. (see page 2)
KEELAND J. E. Andover, B. V. (see page 2)
RHODES T. E. Car Station, Main (see page 7)

Civil Engineer and Surveyor.

Hayward George H. Boston road, P. D.

Clothing and Furnishings.

Bradley J. M. Main (furnishings)
BURKE PATRICK, Village, A. V. (see page 20)
Dean John W. Main
HANNON P. J. (furnishings) Main (see first cover)

Coal and Wood.

CHANDLER GEORGE W. office at J. H. Chandler's, Main (see red page C)
GLEASON FRANK E. office Main c. Essex (see red p. B)
HAYWARD HENRY M. High, B. V. (see page 2)

Confectionery, Fruit, Etc.

Bacigalupo L. J. & Co. Main
Campion J. H. & Co. Main c. Central
JOYCE P. V. Tewksbury, B. V. (see page 2)
KEELAND J. E. Andover, B. V. (see page 2)
RHODES T. E. Car Station, Main (see page 7)
TRULAND WILLIAM F. Essex, A. V. (see adv. index)

Cordage.

McLAWLIN HENRY, Main (see inside last cover)

Crockery and Glassware.

HOLT T. A. & CO. Central (see page 28)
SMITH & MANNING, Essex (see page 28)

Curtains and Fixtures.

Noyes H. P. Park
SMITH & MANNING, Essex (see page 28)

Dentists.

GILBERT CHARLES H. office Bank bldg. Main (see p. 49)
HULME ALBERT E. office over store of J. H. Chandler (see page 56)

Depot Carriages.

Daly Michael J. Main
Shattuck Scott, Main
TUTTLE B. B. Park (see page 4)

Dining Rooms.

RHODES T. E. Car Station (see page 7)
Wiggin George W. Central

Dressmakers.

Abbott Hannah B. Bartlet c. Chestnut
Bodwell Myra J. Maple av.
BURKE ANNIE, Village, A. V. (see page 20)
Carter James O. Mrs.
Chandler Laura M. Elm near Walnut
Collins Mary E. Summer
Donovan Katie E. Brook
Fortis S. Annie, F. V.
Glidden Jane A. Elm
Hayward Gertrude A. Boston road, P. D.
Holt Lizzie, Main, P. D.
Howard Mary J. Post Office av.
Mears Catherine Mrs. Tewksbury, B. V.
McCullough Isabel, Brook, B. V.
Norris Nellie, Summer
Rea Grace, Park
Rhodes E. Alice, North Main
Sanborn M. E. P. 73 Main
Whitney E. A. Mrs. Bartlet c. Morton
Woodbridge M. E. rooms over H. McLawlin's, Main

Drugs and Medicines.

Bliss Arthur, Main
Parker George H. Main
SHATTUCK CHARLES H., M. D. B. V. (see page 76)

Dry and Fancy Goods.

Brown & Shattuck, Main
BURKE PATRICK, Village, A. V. (see page 20)
DALY P. J. Elm square (see red page C)
GREENE & WOODLIN, Andover, B. V. (see over adv. ind.)
Haynes F. G. & Co. Andover, B. V.
HOLT T. A. & CO. Central c. Essex (see page 28)
Ramsdell M. L. Mrs. Park
SMITH & MANNING, Essex (see page 28)

Electric Light Company.

Andover Electric Co. W. H. Coleman supt.

Express Companies.

AMERICAN EXPRESS CO. N. G. Gleason agent, Elm sq. (see adv. index)
BROWN'S ANDOVER AND BOSTON EXPRESS, B. B. Tuttle prop. Park (see page 4)
O'DONNELL HUGH, Ballard Vale (see adv. index)

Fish, Oysters, Etc.

FARMER THOMAS J. Post Office av. (see page 20)
Hutchinson J. E. North Main
KEELAND J. E. Andover, B. V. (see page 2)

Florists.

Lockhart James, High
Millett George D. Holt District
Mitchell Henry, Jenkins' Corner, H. D.
PIDDINGTON GEORGE, School (see page 7)
PLAYDON JOHN H. F. V. (see adv. index)
Shattuck Caroline A. Mrs. S. D.

Flour, Feed and Grain.

Campion J. H. & Co. Main c. Essex
DALY P. J. Elm square (see red page C)
GREENE & WOODLIN, Andover, B. V. (see over adv. index)
Haynes F. G. & Co. Andover, B. V.
HOLT T. A. & CO. Central c. Essex (see page 28)
SMITH & MANNING, Essex (see page 28)

Furniture.

Noyes H. P. Park
Shawsheen Furniture Co. Andover, B. V.

Grocers.

Campion J. H. & Co. Main c. Essex
DALY P. J. Elm square (see red page C)
GREENE & WOODLIN, Andover, B. V. (see over adv. index)
Haynes F. G. & Co. Andover, B. V.
HOLT T. A. & CO. Central c. Essex (see page 28)
SMITH & MANNING, Essex (see page 28)

Hair Dressers.

Bean J. M. Town Hall
Ledwell William, Park
Miller Granville A. 2 Pearson
Soehrens John H. Main
Stewart John, Chapman block, Main

Hardware and Cutlery.

McLAWLIN HENRY, Main (see inside last cover)

Harness Makers.

Mayer George A. Park
Shattuck Charles H. Main

Hats and Caps.

Bradley J. H. Main
Dean J. William, Main

Horseshoers.

ANDERSON & BOWMAN, Park c. Bartlet (see page 99)
HARRIMAN THOMAS P. Park (see page 4)
Sweeney Dennis, Pearson

Hotels.

ELM HOUSE, Elm square, C. F. Gruber prop. (see page 18)
Mansion House, Chapel av. E. P. Hitchcock prop.

Ice Cream.

Hinton Allen, South Main, S. D.
KEELAND J. E. Andover, B. V. (see page 2)
Murphy Thomas, Main
RHODES T. E. Car Station, Main (see page 7)
Wiggin George W. Central

Ice Dealers.

HAYWARD HENRY M. High, B. V. (see page 2)
Holt Brooks F. Main, S. D.

Insurance Agents and Companies.

Merrimack Mutual Fire Ins. Co. office Bank bldg. J. A. Smart
  secretary
Rogers Barnett, office Main c. Central

Job Printers.

THE ANDOVER PRESS, (limited) J. N. Cole manager
  (see page 86)

Justices of the Peace.

Boutwell Fred E. West District
Kimball John F. School
Marland Charles H. Ballard Vale
Rogers Barnett, Main
Smart Joseph A. Main (see also lawyers)

Laundries.

AMERICAN HAND LAUNDRY, Main, Mrs. M. A. Hodges prop. (see page 12)
American Steam Laundry, Park

Livery and Boarding Stables.

Daly Michael J. Main
ELM HOUSE STABLES, W. H. Higgins prop. (see red page A)
Pray John, Main
Wardwell Joseph W. Lowell, B. V.

Lumber Dealers.

CUMMINGS BRAINARD, Park (see inside last cover)
Hardy & Cole, Essex
HAYWARD HENRY M. High, B. V. (see page 2)
MASON C. B. Old Abbott Store bldg. Main (see red page B)

Machinist.

CHASE HERBERT F. Post Office av. (see page 16)

Manufacturers.

Bradlee Mills, B. V. (flannels)
Barnard Henry W. Post Office av. (shoes and slippers)
Brown Benjamin, Main (shoes and slippers)
Colquhoun John H., W. P. (hosiery)
Craighead & Kintz Mfg. Co. B. V. (lamps and art work)
Donald W. C. & Co. Main, F. V. (ink and blacking)
Edwards Henry, river road, W. P. (machine brushes)
Emerson Soap Co. G. F. Holt prop. W. P. (soap powder)
Hardy Charles A. Lowell, W. P. (brushes)
Hardy & Cole, Essex (boxes)
Jaquith Newton, Main, S. D. (boots and shoes)
Ladd H. P., B. V. (boxes)
Marland Mills (M. T. Stevens & Son) M. V. (flannels)
POOR WILLIAM, Main, F. V. (wagons and carts) (see p. 26)
Smith & Dove Mfg. Co. (shoe and carpet thread)
TYER RUBBER CO. Main (rubber goods and druggists' sundries) (see red page A)

Masons and Builders.

Gleason Moses V. Maple av.
Howard Timothy, North Main
McCarthy John, 2d, Pearson
Ross William R. Centre, B. V.
WHITE M. E. Essex (see last cover)

Meat and Provisions.

Brown William G. High
Eames Lemuel H. Elm
SHERRY R. J. Tewksbury, B. V. (see page 100)
Stark John S. Andover, B. V.
VALPEY BROTHERS, Main (see page 87)
WAKEFIELD JOHN P. Main c. Park (see page 12)

Milkmen.

Dodson Richard, High, F. V.
Foster Francis H. Central
Foster George E. 32 Salem
Gould Milo H., S. D.
Jones Samuel M. off Main, S. D.
Playdon Alfred G. Lowell, F. V.
Shattuck Frederick H., S. D.
Stone Charles N. L. High, F. V.
Ward Richard A. Lowell, F. V.

Milliners.

Brown & Shattuck, Main
Gibson Rebecca R. Mrs. Lowell, B. V.
Howard Mary J. Post Office av.
Neal O. W. Miss, Draper's block, Main

Music Teachers.

Boynton Clara R., W. P. (piano and organ)
CHANDLER MARION R. High (piano) (see page 3)
Cole Maud M. Chestnut (piano)
Jarvie Margaret, Abbot (piano)
RHODES T. E. 19 North Main (piano and organ) (see p. 7)
Sanborn C. H. A. Miss, Morton (piano)
Scammon A. Leland Miss

Newsdealers.

Chandler John H. Main
Marland Charles H. Ballard Vale

Newspaper.

THE ANDOVER TOWNSMAN, J. N. Cole manager (see page 86)

Notary Public.

FOSTER GEORGE W. office Bank bldg. Main (see p. 47)

Nurses.

Kinley Jesse Mrs. Poor, F. V.
Moody Sarah M. Ballard Vale

Orchestras.

Andover Band Orchestra, A. Bliss agent
ANDOVER ORCHESTRA, O. P. Chase pres. and manager (see page 4)

Optical Goods.

WHITING J. E. Barnard block, Main (see page 12)

Painters and Paper Hangers.

Barnard Edwin H. Essex
Caldwell A. W. High
DAVIS GEORGE E. 50 Salem (see page 12)
Meader Samuel, Porter
Reed William J. Elm
ROWE E. J. Post Office av. (see last cover)
Shaw John B Tewksbury road
Winton David J. Centre, B. V.
Wood William, Park
Young Levi C. off Main

Paints, Oils, Glass, Etc.

Barnard Edwin H. Essex
McLawlin Henry, Main

Paper Hangings.

Ramsdell Harry A. Park
ROWE E. J. Post Office av. (see last cover)
SMITH & MANNING, Essex (see page 28)

Photographer.

Newman Charles H. Bartlet

Physicians.

ABBOTT CHARLES E., M. D. office 43 Main (see p. 29)
Leitch John A., M. D. office Barnard block, Main
Richards James F., M. D. office Main c. Punchard av.
Sanborn Miss E. M. E., M. D. Morton
SCOTT C. W., M. D. office Main near Punchard av. (see page 75)
SHATTUCK CHARLES H., M. D., B. V. (see page 76)

Picture Frames, Etc.

Ramsdell Harry A. Park

Plumbers.

Pike Erwin C. Park
Saunders George, Main
WALSH M. T. 8 Essex (see page 5)

Real Estate.

Cole George S. Central
CUMMINGS CHARLES O. Elm c. Washington av. (see page 25)
Rogers Barnett, Main c. Essex

Sewer and Drain Pipe.

McLAWLIN HENRY, Main (see inside last cover)
Pike E. Park

Sewing Machines.

Ramsdell M. L. Park

Silver and Plated Ware.

WHITING J. E. Barnard block, Main (see page 12)

Sporting Goods.

CHASE H. F. Post Office av. (see page 16)
McLAWLIN HENRY, Main (see inside last cover)
WHITING J. E. Main (see page 12)

Stoves, Ranges, Etc.

Pike Erwin, Park
Saunders George, Main
WALSH M. P. 8 Essex (see page 5)

Tailors.

Bradley Joseph M. Main
Dean J. William, Main
HANNON P. J. Main (see first cover)

Teaming and Jobbing.

Buck Silas, Marland, B. V.
CHANDLER GEORGE W. office at J. H. Chandler's (see red page C)
Rea Charles P. Park near Florence
Stack Michael J. Pearson
Simons Fred, Salem near Prospect Hill, H. D.
TUTTLE B. B. (baggage express) office Park (see page 4)

Tinsmiths.

Pike Erwin, Park
Saunders George, Main
WALSH M. T. 8 Essex (see page 5)

Undertaker.

MESSER FRANK H. Park (see page 18)

Upholsterers.

Dinsmore Frank A. Park
Noyes H. P. Park

Variety Stores.

Chapman Ovid, Main
Mitchell Annie D., F. V.
Murphy Thomas, Main
TRULAND WILLIAM F. Essex, A. V. (see page 26)

Watches and Jewelry.

WHITING J. E. Barnard block, Main (see page 12)

Wheelwrights.

O'Connell John, Park
POOR WILLIAM, Main, F. V. (see page 26)

Wood Dealers.

CHANDLER GEORGE W. office J. H. Chandler's (see red page C)
GLEASON FRANK E. office Main c. Essex (see red p. B)
HAYWARD HENRY M., B. V. (see page 2)
Pillsbury George P. Ballard Vale

American Express Company.

FORWARDERS TO ALL PARTS OF THE WORLD.

Local Office, Elm Square.

Service between BOSTON, NEW YORK, SOUTH and WEST
UNEXCELLED.

SIXTEEN TRAINS DAILY.
  From Boston: 7.30, 10.25, 12.00 A. M., 12.30, 2.15, 3.20, 5.00 and 7.00 P. M.
  From the East and North: Due in Andover, 7.39, 7.46, 10.33, 11.10 A. M., 12.16, 12.37, 4.25, 7.11 P. M.

Money Orders.   Travelers' Cheques.   Money Transferred by Telegraph.

N. G. GLEASON, Agent.

ANDERSON & BOWMAN,
HORSE SHOERS
—AND—
JOBBERS.

All kinds of Interfering and Overreaching Horses Shod on Scientific Principles.

CARRIAGE WORK
Of all kinds done at short notice.

SHOP, PARK STREET,   ANDOVER, MASS.

HUGH O'DONNELL,
—PROPRIETOR—

Ballard Vale & Lawrence
EXPRESS.

Lawrence Office, 473 Essex St.
Boston Office, 30 Court Square.

Transferring to all parts of the United States and Canada, and all other parts of the world.

Ballard Vale Office, Center St.

JOHN H. PLAYDEN,
—Florist—
—AND—

Grower of Early Vegetable Plants.
CUT FLOWERS,
Floral Designs, &c.
Chrysanthemums in Endless Variety.
CHOICE PANSIES OUR SPECIALTY.
Greenhouse, Lowell Street, Frye Village.

R. J. SHERRY,
—DEALER IN—

Choice Meats and Provisions.
VEGETABLES OF ALL KINDS IN THEIR SEASON.

Tewksbury Street,   *Near Depot,*
BALLARD VALE.

"The only advertising medium for Andover."

✢ THE ✢
ANDOVER TOWNSMAN.
ANDOVER, MASS.

PUBLISHED BY

THE ANDOVER PRESS,
The LEADING PRINTERS of ESSEX COUNTY.

JOHN N. COLE, Treasurer and Manager.

FRANK E. GLEASON,

(Successor to JOHN CORNELL,)

—DEALER IN—

COAL, ✳ ✳
WOOD, ✳
HAY ✳
✳ STRAW.

Office, CARTER'S BUILDING, *Main Street.*
Coal Yard, Railroad Street, near Freight Station.
ANDOVER.

C. B. MASON,
Contractor and Builder, ✦ ✦ Andover, Mass.
Plans of Cottages furnished. Builders' Supplies in stock. Repairing in all its branches.
Shop and Yard, Old Abbott Store Building, Main Street.
RESIDENCE, ABBOT STREET.

P. J. DALY,
—— DEALER IN ——

Dry Goods
—AND—
Groceries,
Boots, Shoes and Rubbers
Of all Descriptions,

At Reasonable Prices.

CHOICE BRANDS FLOUR.
GRAIN.
Crockery, Glassware,
And everything usually found in a General Store.

THE NEW BLOCK, ELM SQUARE.

G. W. CHANDLER,
—— DEALER IN ——

COAL AND WOOD.

All the best qualities of **ANTHRACITE COAL** *constantly on hand.*
All orders for Cumberland and Lehigh Coal will receive prompt attention.

TEAMING AND JOBBING
Of all kinds done by experienced men, at short notice.

Office at J. H. Chandler's Periodical Store,
Main Street, Andover.

C

Artistic Clothing!

That which adapts itself perfectly to the form and gratifies the taste is the kind we are now displaying.

Everything New, Stylish and Attractive,

And added to that a guarantee of durability.

DO YOU NEED a SUIT or OVERCOAT?

If you do, and you have not made up your mind as to its character, come and see us, and let our offerings decide you.

HAMEL & CLOUTIER,

——DEALERS IN——

Fine Clothing, Gents' Furnishings, Hats,
TRUNKS, VALISES, ETC.

405 ESSEX STREET,   LAWRENCE.
(Sign of the Golden Trunk.)

D

BUILDERS'   **SUPPLIES.**

New Brick Factory on Winter Street,

Near Boston and Maine Passenger Station,

LAWRENCE, MASS.

E

✻ TREAT ✻
HARDWARE AND SUPPLY CO.

Headquarters for

HARDWARE, CUTLERY,

✻ Cordage, ✻

PAINTS, OILS,

IRON
—AND—
STEEL,

—ALSO,—

Blacksmiths', Carpenters' and Machinists'

TOOLS,

—AND—

MILL SUPPLIES.

582 & 584 Essex Street, Lawrence, Mass.

J. M. SMITH, General Manager.

F

✢ ESTABLISHED 1876 ✢
— BY —
FRANK EMERSON.

Compounding Physicians' Prescriptions made a Specialty
AT ALL HOURS, DAY OR NIGHT.

A competent person in attendance at night to answer all calls of necessity. This DEPARTMENT is complete, and while the best service is rendered, the prices are consistent.

A LARGE STOCK OF

Fancy Goods, Patent Medicines,
HOMEOPATHIC REMEDIES,

Pocket • Cutlery, • Razors • and • Scissors,

CONFECTIONERY AND CIGARS, WINES AND LIQUORS,

*Trusses, Elastic Hose, Shoulder Braces,
Supporters, Suspensory Bandages, Crutches,
Hot Water Bottles or Bags, Ice Bags,
All sorts of Syringes, Urinals, Bed Pans,
Baker's Douches, Atomizers, &c.*

PROPRIETARY ARTICLES.

Emerson's Worm Syrup, Sarsaparilla, Glycerine Lotion, Botanic Cough Syrup, Vegetable Liver Pills, Cyclone Corn Cure, Beef, Wine and Iron, and Carbolic Healing Salve.

122 BROADWAY, SOUTH LAWRENCE, MASS.

C

N. S. S. TOMPKINS,
(Successor to TOMPKINS & MANN,)

PAINTS,
OILS,
VARNISHES,
Chemicals
—AND—
Dye-Stuffs.

191 ESSEX STREET, LAWRENCE.

GEO. W. COLBURN & CO.

✳ ART ✳ NOVELTIES.	Practical Gilders
ALBUMS —AND— BIBLES.	—AND— PICTURE FRAME MAKERS.
Old Engravings Carefully Restored.	A choice line of Engravings, Etchings, Water Color Paintings, Etc., constantly on hand.
	STATIONERS AND FANCY GOODS DEALERS.

281 Essex St., Lawrence, Mass.

H

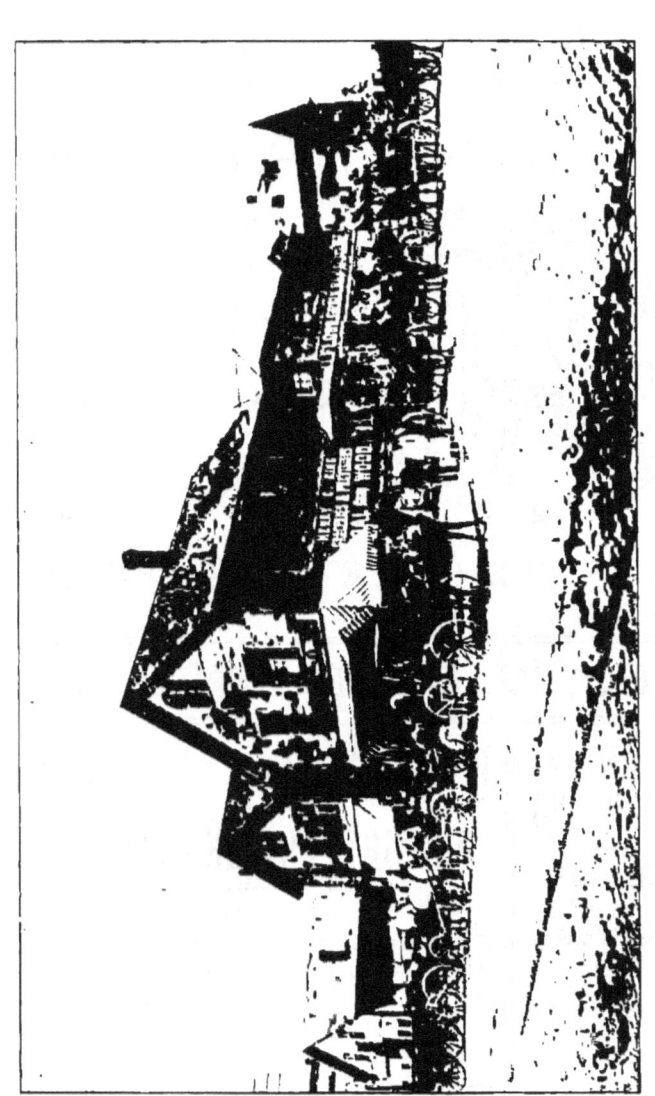

HENRY C. KING, 106 SOUTH BROADWAY, LAWRENCE. (See also page K.)

(Continued from opposite page.)

HENRY C. KING,
— DEALER IN —

CHOICE FAMILY GROCERIES
— AND —
PROVISIONS,
Wood, Coal, Hay, Grain,
LIME AND CEMENT,

Also, Wheat, Barley, Scraps, Oyster Shells, etc.

Prepared Wood and Kindlings.

106 South Broadway, Lawrence, Mass.

Telephone No. 200.

Goods delivered in Andover and North Andover.

(See also opposite page, I.)

Enterprise Portrait Co.,
LAWRENCE, MASS.,

Enlarge Small Pictures
To any size, and finish in

India Ink, Water Colors, Crayon or Oil,
Cheaper, Better, Quicker, than any Copying House in Essex County.

We Guarantee Our Work to be of the Finest Quality.
We keep a full line of

ELEGANT ✧ PORTRAIT ✧ FRAMES
Constantly on hand, and also make

Picture Frames of all kinds to order.

Don't be humbugged by out-of-town parties, but patronize Lawrence industries and deal with a reliable house,

THE ENTERPRISE.
We kindly invite you to visit our Studio at

116 BROADWAY,   LAWRENCE.
Enterprise Portrait Co.

K

KENNELLY & SYLVESTER,
PIANOS AND ORGANS
For Cash or Easy Payments.

Old Instruments Taken in Exchange.

We have a large stock of

MUSIC AND SMALL MUSICAL MERCHANDISE.

We are prepared to do

PIANO

AND

ORGAN

TUNING,

Repairing,

Polishing,

ETC.,

Including

Church Organs,

At short notice and reasonable rates.

CALL ON US AT

248 & 250 ESSEX STREET, LAWRENCE.

L

H. J. TREES' CLOTHES CLEANSING WORKS.
(Established 1849.)

Ladies' or Gents' Garments **CLEANSED OR DYED** in the best possible manner.

Office, 473 Essex Street,
Next to Bicknell Bros.' Store.

DYE HOUSE, 133 LAWRENCE STREET, LAWRENCE, MASS.

TREES' STEAM MACHINE
CARPET BEATING WORKS.
133 Lawrence Street.
Office, 473 Essex Street, Lawrence, Mass.

Carpets Taken Up, Beaten & Laid.

The Only Steam Carpet Machine in the City.

Every Carpet Beaten Separately.

Blankets and Quilts Cleansed.
FEATHER BEDS RENOVATED.
M

THE NEW T. D. HALLEY
GREENHOUSE!
338 & 340 Broadway, Lawrence, Mass.

Cut Flowers,
Floral Designs,
PLANTS,

And everything that a FIRST-CLASS GREENHOUSE keeps for sale.

PRICES THE LOWEST.

Goods delivered in the Andovers free.

Electric cars pass the door.

J. B. HALLEY, Proprietor.

BOUQUET.
210 Essex Street, Lawrence, Mass.

MILLINERY.

A large stock of
TRIMMED MILLINERY
Constantly on hand.

Special attention given Andover patrons.

Mrs. E. C. MONK.

BOSTON STORE.

WILLIAM OSWALD & CO.

Headquarters for

DRY GOODS,
CARPETS,
UPHOLSTERY,
MILLINERY,

—AND—

GENTS' FURNISHING GOODS.

We carry the

✦ LARGEST ✦ ASSORTMENT ✦

In each department of any store outside of Boston.

The Secret of Our Great Success is

HONEST GOODS AT LOW PRICES!

When in want of anything in our line, be sure and give us a call. We can save you money on every purchase.

The only COMPLETE DRY GOODS ESTABLISHMENT in the city.

Don't forget to visit our basement, where we carry a

MAMMOTH STOCK OF

House Furnishings at Popular Low Prices!

WILLIAM OSWALD & CO.,

225, 227, 229, 231, 233 & 235 ESSEX STREET,

LAWRENCE, MASS.

O

HUGO E. DICK,

Plain and Ornamental

JOB ✲ PRINTER.

Color Work a Specialty.

Also, Publisher of

"THE ANZEIGER,"

The only GERMAN NEWSPAPER in Essex and Middlesex Counties.

EIGHT LARGE PAGES of Interesting German Reading for only

$1.00 A YEAR.

118 Essex Street, Lawrence, Mass.

GOULD'S
BAY STATE DYE WORKS.

Ladies' and Gents' Clothing

Dyed, Cleansed and Finished at short notice and in a first-class manner.

KID GLOVES AND FEATHERS A SPECIALTY.

164 Essex Street, Lawrence, Mass.

D. M. LEARY. S. E. GOULD.

PRICES
AT THE
BARGAIN ✲ EMPORIUM
ARE
The Lowest in New England!
FOR

Millinery, Dry Goods and Notions, Boots and Shoes, Patent Medicines and Toilet Articles, Crockery and House-Furnishing Goods.

L. C. MOORE & CO.,
302, 304, 308 & 310 ESSEX STREET,
LAWRENCE, MASS.

P

WHEN ABOUT TO FURNISH A HOUSE
CALL AT THE
Largest Furniture and Carpet Store
IN LAWRENCE.

Four Floors and Basement, covering more than 20,000 Square Feet of Floor Space.

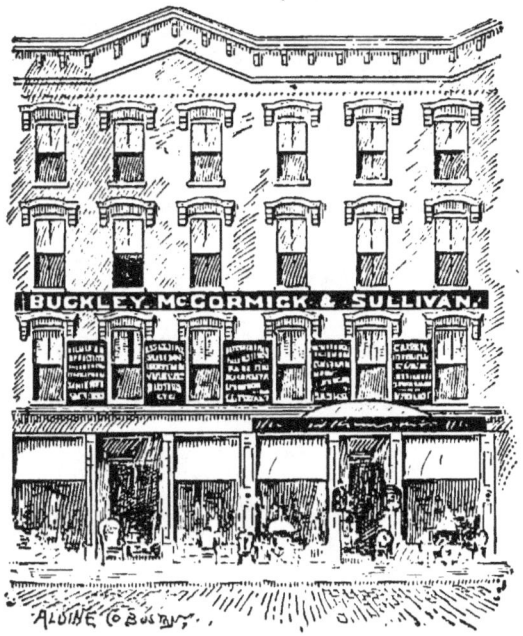

We carry the LARGEST STOCK and LATEST DESIGNS, in FIRST-CLASS HOUSE-FURNISHING GOODS to be found outside of Boston. Our line of CARPETS, LACE CURTAINS, UPHOLSTERY and DRAPERY CLOTHS are unexcelled. We also keep several first-class Upholsterers, and MANUFACTURE all of our UPHOLSTERED FURNITURE. Repairing done at short notice and at low prices, by

BUCKLEY, McCORMICK & SULLIVAN,
218, 220 & 222 ESSEX STREET, LAWRENCE, MASS.

Q

MAX NIDETCH,
CUSTOM * TAILOR.

Suits made to order in all the leading styles at reasonable prices.
Always in stock,
Ready-Made Clothing
—FOR—
Men, Boys and Women.
Cleaning, Repairing, Dyeing and Pressing
AT SHORT NOTICE.

114 ESSEX STREET,   LAWRENCE, MASS.

M. A. KEYES,
Fashionable * Millinery,
Feathers, Trimmings, &c.
KINDLY FAVOR US WITH AN INSPECTION.

103 & 105 Essex Street, Lawrence, Mass.

JOHN SLATER,
PRACTICAL PLUMBER AND COPPERSMITH.
DEALER IN
Model Ranges, Furnaces,
—AND—
KITCHEN FURNISHING GOODS.
Oil Stoves a Specialty.
Plumber's Work in all branches done by experienced workmen.
Cor. Essex and Hampshire Streets, Lawrence.

R

1878   **1893**

E. C. STIEGLER & CO.,

UPHOLSTERERS

—— AND ——

Furniture Dealers.

Fine Custom Work and Repairing all kinds of Furniture.

Special attention given to

REPAIRING & POLISHING ANTIQUE FURNITURE.

The Puritan Spring

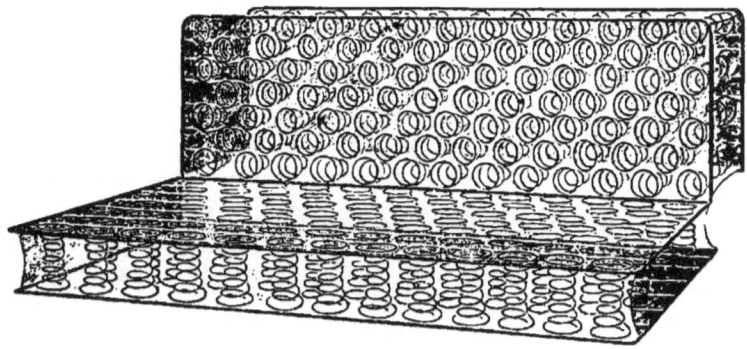

Contains 176 springs. We also carry a large assortment of other leading styles, and Bedding of all kinds. A general line of good

FURNITURE

Will always be found at our store, at very low prices.

Goods called for and delivered in all parts of Andover, North Andover and vicinity.

124 ESSEX STREET, CORNER MILL,
LAWRENCE, MASS.

S

Offices and Prices on Ground Floor! *First-class Workmanship Only.*

NEAT PRINTING - -

· · · · · Is the Kind You Want.

WORK THAT IS DONE IN A SLOVENLY MANNER, FOR A CHEAP PRICE, IS NOT THE KIND THAT PAYS EITHER THE CONSUMER OR THE PRINTER. . .

We have the facilities to turn out—and DO turn out—a VERY FINE GRADE OF PRINTING, at A REASONABLE PRICE.

Address all orders for Printing to - - -

Wm. G. Merrill,
Geo. H. Goldsmith.

TELEGRAM PRINTING HOUSE,

25 & 27 Appleton Street, Lawrence, Mass.

❖ FRANK A. WARREN.

CLOTHING DEALER.

Men's and Boys' Clothing,
Hats, Caps, Underwear,
Gloves, Hosiery,
Umbrellas, &c.

HORSE BLANKETS AND ROBES.

Largest line of TRUNKS in Essex County. Sole agent for the celebrated

CLINTON WALL TRUNK.

The CLINTON can be opened without moving from the wall. Saves damaging the plastering or tearing the carpet.

❖ **187 ESSEX STREET, Lawrence.**

T

Banquet, Piano, Chandelier, Hanging and Table

We make a specialty of

Silk Shades, WIRE Shade Frames —AND— Anything in this line.

BALL & MULLEN
275 Essex Street,
LAWRENCE, MASS.

The Largest and Best Equipped

WALL PAPER
and
WINDOW SHADE
HOUSE IN ESSEX COUNTY.

REMEMBER, anything in this line we can furnish you with.

✻ SEE US? ✻

U

A. W. Stearns & Co.

309 & 311 Essex St., 270 Common St., Lawrence.

Dress Goods, Silks, Trimmings. Velvets, Fancy Goods, Ribbons, Laces,	Underwear, Hosiery, Blankets, Flannels, Cloakings, Furs, Garments.

"A man who does not know how to learn from his mistakes turns the best schoolmaster out of his life."—*Henry Ward Beecher.*

Possibly, during our existence as a dry goods firm, we have made some mistakes —everybody does. However, instead of blindly pursuing the same course, we have avoided all similar circumstances, and as a result we stand to-day at the head of the class in the Dry-Goods, Cloak and Carpet business.

Here are two mammoth stores, one on Essex street, the other on Common street; nearly 40,000 square feet of floor surface. The two buildings are so connected that they form one great establishment, which for architectural beauty, modern conveniences and business facilities is so far in advance of any other in this vicinity as to completely out-class them all.

An elevator takes you to every floor.

A patented electric cable cash railway "scoots" off with the money, and is back with the change in a jiffy.

Every department is a small store in itself.

Three floors for Carpets, one for Cloaks, and half of another for Underwear— that's the scale that our business is conducted on; you'll find it so if you investigate.

In Dress Novelties we lead. In Garments we lead. In everything we lead. No use to particularize. We are *leaders*, EXPERTS, MASTERS in every branch of the business.

But do you for an instant imagine that we could gain this eminence if the goods, the prices and the treatment were not as they should be?

We'll sell anything in our line as low as anybody in the business—lower, if we can.

We will not handle doubtful goods.

Our clerks are courteous and attentive.

A. W. Stearns & Co.

309 & 311 Essex St., 270 Common St., Lawrence.

v

FRENCH, PUFFER & CO.,

HEADQUARTERS FOR

Solid Silver & Plated Ware.

We also have
A Great Variety
—OF—
DINNER,
Tea,
TOILET
—AND—
LEMONADE
SETS.

HANGING TABLE LAMPS

ROGERS BROS.' 1847

KNIVES, FORKS AND SPOONS

A Specialty.

WE CARRY A LARGE STOCK,

Giving our customers a good variety to choose from.

—ALSO,—

Vases, Ornaments, &c.

A full line of

WHITE WARE

ALWAYS ✣ IN ✣ STOCK.

389 Essex Street, Lawrence, Mass.

ARCHILLE VALLEY,
✤ *Photographer,* ✤

390 Essex Street, Lawrence.

Small Pictures enlarged to any size and done in INDIA INK or CRAYON PORTRAIT, SOLAR PRINTS, BROMIDES, and OIL FERROTYPES.

Cabinets $2.50 a dozen.

One dozen Extra Finish Panels, including one 16 by 20 Crayon Portrait, for $3.50.

4 Tintypes for 50 cents.

W

A. F. RYDER,

Registered & Pharmacist,

Cor. Essex Street and Broadway,

LAWRENCE, MASS.

G. W. DODSON,
—DEALER IN—
STOVES, RANGES, FURNACES,
Etc., Etc.
PLUMBING,
Steam, Water and Gas Pipe Fitting.
—ALSO,—
Agent for the ARLINGTON RANGE and ECONOMY COMBINATION HOT-WATER and HOT-AIR HEATERS.

11 Lawrence Street. Lawrence, Mass.

IF YOU WANT ANYTHING IN
CROCKERY ❋ WARE,
In GLASS WARE,
In WOODEN WARE,
• In FIBRE WARE,
In TIN WARE,
Or in GRANITE IRON WARE,
—CALL UPON—
SULLIVAN & WILLARD,
531 ESSEX STREET, LAWRENCE.

X

WILLIAM P. REGAN,

Architect

OFFICE,

Rooms 1 & 2, Essex Bank Building,

ESSEX STREET,

Lawrence.

Residence, Pearson Street, Andover.

C. A. LAWRENCE & SON,
Portrait and View Photographers.

ALL STYLES OF

Photographs and Ferrotypes.

A SPECIALTY MADE OF

Views of ANDOVER  NORTH ANDOVER.

Satisfaction Guaranteed to All.

181 ESSEX STREET, LAWRENCE, MASS.

NEW HIGH ARM NO. 9
WHEELER & WILSON SEWING MACHINE.

BEST ON EARTH.

Easy, Simple, Durable, Light - Running, and Noiseless.
It runs forward and backward without breaking the thread.
We have machines from $5.00 to $50.00.
Call and examine our stock before purchasing elsewhere.

375 Essex Street,   Lawrence, Mass.

Y

THORNTON BROS.,
FLORISTS.

Fancy Roses.

DESIGNS FOR FUNERALS A SPECIALTY.

Choice Cut Flowers
OF EVERY VARIETY.

PALMS AND DECORATIVE PLANTS.

Trees, Bulbs and Seeds.

Largest Greenhouse in New England.
PRICES VERY LOW.
GOODS DELIVERED IN THE ANDOVERS.

THORNTON BROS.,
384 BROADWAY,   LAWRENCE, MASS.
Telephone.

Z

EDWARD H. HUMPHREY,
(Successor to HUMPHREY BROS.,)

—DEALER IN—

COAL and WOOD.

CITY OFFICE,
56 North Union Street.
OFFICE AND YARD,
9 South Union Street,
LAWRENCE.

COAL for DOMESTIC USE.

PHILADELPHIA & READING
Free Burning White Ash,
Best Franklin,
Shamokin.

LEHIGH & WILKESBARRE COAL CO.'S
Egg, Stove and Broken sizes always in stock.

—ALSO—

Best George's Creek Cumberland,
For Blacksmith and Steam Use.

Dry Slab and Spruce Wood,
By the Cord, Load or Basket.

All Goods Delivered in North Andover at Lawrence Prices.

Electric cars pass the office.   Telephone No. 229-6.

A A

WILLIAM FORBES & SON,

CONTRACTORS FOR

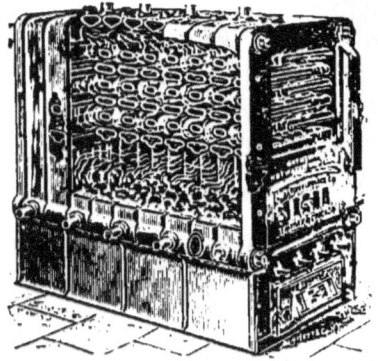

PLUMBING, HOT-WATER & STEAM HEATING,

—AND DEALER IN—

PLUMBERS' ✳ SUPPLIES.

450 Essex Street, Lawrence.

⇢ SINGER ⇠

SEWING ✢ MACHINE

OFFICE,

29 Franklin Street, Lawrence.

G. C. HUTCHINSON, - MANAGER.

✢ SUPPLIES ✢

OF ALL KINDS

AT WHOLESALE AND RETAIL.

B B

TAYLOR & CO.,

Wholesale and Retail Dealers in

CHOICE FAMILY GROCERIES,

Meats and Provisions,

CANNED GOODS, COUNTRY PRODUCE,

Hay, Grain and Straw.

Below you will find a few of our many specialties:

POTATOES
—AND—
SWEET POTATOES.
You will always find in our stock a good selection of both.

BUTTER.
We are large receivers of Dairy and Creamery Butter, in all sizes from half-pound prints to fifty-pound tubs.

CHEESE.
We always keep on hand an assortment of Cheese, including Pineapple, Edam, Young America, Neufchatel, Cream, &c.

FLOUR.
We are millers' agents for "PILLSBURY'S BEST XXXX," the quality of which is known not only in this country but across the water.

FRESH EGGS.
We have a contract with several large heneries, which furnish us with STRICTLY FRESH EGGS all the year round.

LARD.
We always keep the best—the pure leaf. We have it in three and five-pound pails and ten-pound tubs. We also keep cheaper grades.

MEATS.
We have as nice a line of MEATS AND PROVISIONS as can be found in Essex county.

TEAS.
We can suit you on Teas. We have all grades of Oolong and Japan Teas, also English Breakfast, Gunpowder, and Uncolored Japan.

COFFEES.
We keep the best Coffee at all times. One trial makes a regular customer. Our trade in this line increases each year.

Don't forget to call when in town.

57 to 61 Broadway, corner Common Street,

Opposite B. & M. Railroad Station,

LAWRENCE.

Handy to Electric Cars.

C C

JOHN WURZBACHER.   ERNEST RUPF.

WURZBACHER & CO.,
Stoves, Ranges, Furnaces,

LAMPS,

Kitchen Furnishing

Goods, &c.,

PLUMBING,

Gas and Water Piping,

TIN, COPPER AND SHEET IRON WORKERS.

STOVE REPAIRS AND ALL KINDS OF JOBBING ATTENDED TO.

Agents for BAY STATE RANGES.

17 and 21 Jackson & 162 Common Streets,

LAWRENCE, MASS.

JAMES DORMAN,
Mason, Contractor and Builder.

PLANS, SPECIFICATIONS AND ESTIMATES

FURNISHED FOR

Buildings of Brick or Stone,

OF ANY STYLE OF ARCHITECTURE.

Hand & Steam Derricks and Engines

TO LET.

RESIDENCE, 116 CROSS STREET,

Lawrence, Mass.

D D

THE OLDEST AND Largest Grocery House IN LAWRENCE.

Established 1860.

FIRST-CLASS GOODS AT FAIR PRICES.

J. M. CURRIER & CO.,
Wholesale and Retail Grocers,
MEAT AND PROVISION DEALERS.

87 Essex, 17 and 19 Newbury Streets, Lawrence, Mass.

We deliver goods in North Andover every day.

Index to Lawrence Patrons.

Ball & Mullen, wall paper, shades, lamps, etc. 275 Essex......page U
Briggs & Allyn Mfg. Co. builders' supplies................page E
Buckley, McCormick & Sullivan, furniture, 222 Essex........page Q
Clark Charles & Son, druggists, 179 Essex..............card inset
Colburn G. W. & Co. art novelties, frames, gilders and makers,
   281 Essex...page H
Currier J. M. & Co. grocers and provision dealers, 87 Essex. top this page
Dick Hugo E. job printer, 118 Essex......................page P
Dodson G. W. stoves, ranges, etc. 11 Lawrence............page X
Dorman James, contractor................................page DD
Emerson Frank, druggist, 122 So. Broadway, So. Lawrence....page G
Enterprise Portrait Co. portraits, frames, etc., 116 Broadway....page K
Fellows S. W. jeweler, pianos, wall paper, etc. 265 Essex......page
Forbes William & Son, plumbers, kitchen furnishings, etc. 450
   Essex ....page BB
French, Puffer & Co. silver and plated ware, lamps, etc. 389
   Essex ....page W
Gould, Bay State Dye Works, office 164 Essex..............page P

EE

INDEX TO LAWRENCE PATRONS—*continued*.

Halley T. D. florist, 338 and 340 Broadway...............page N
Hamel & Cloutier, clothing and men's furnishings, 405 Essex...page D
Humphrey Edward H. coal and wood, 56 North Union.......page AA
Hutchinson G. C. sewing machines, 29 Franklin............page BB
Keyes M. A. millinery, 103 and 105 Essex..................page R
Kennelly & Sylvester, pianos, organs, etc. 248 and 250 Essex...page L
King Henry C. general mdse. 106 So. Broadway, So. Lawrence.page I, K
Lawrence C. A. & Son, photographer, 181 Essex.............page Y
Lord & Co. pianos, organs, musical mdse. 360 Essex..second card inset.
Moore L. C. & Co. general merchandise, 302 Essex..........page P
Nidetch Max, custom tailor, 114 Essex.....................page R
Oswald William & Co. dry and fancy goods, etc. 225-235 Essex..page O
Regan William P. architect, office Essex Bank bldg. Essex......page Y
Ryder A. F. druggist, cor. Essex and Broadway.............page X
Slater John, plumber and coppersmith, Essex cor. Hampshire....page R
Stearns A. W. dry and fancy goods, ladies' garments, etc. Essex..page V
Stiegler E. C. & Co. furniture, upholstering, etc. 124 Essex.....page S
Sullivan & Willard, crockery, glass, tinware, etc. 531 Essex....page X
Taylor & Co. wholesale and retail grocers, 57 to 61 Broadway..page CC
Telegram Printing House, 25 and 27 Appleton...............page T
The Bouquet, millinery, 210 Essex..........................page N
Thornton Brothers, florists, 384 Broadway..................page Z
Tompkins N. S. S. paints, oils, dye stuffs, etc. 191 Essex......page H
Treat Hardware and Supply Co. 582 and 584 Essex...........page F
Trees Steam Machine Carpet Beating Works, 473 Essex......page M
Trees H. J. dye house, office 473 Essex.....................page M
Valley Archille, photographer, 390 Essex...................page W
Warren F. A. men's clothing and furnishings, 187 Essex......page T
Wheeler & Wilson Sewing Machine Co. 375 Essex............page Y
Whitney H. M. & Co. druggists, 297 Essex............first card inset
Wurzbacher & Co. stoves, ranges, etc. 17 and 21 Jackson and
    162 Common...page DD

FRANK M. GREENWOOD,

——DEALER IN——

PURE COCHECIWICK LAKE ICE

Families and Stores Supplied.

Residence, Pond Street, North Andover.

THE
NORTH ANDOVER
DIRECTORY,

———CONTAINING———

A General Directory of the Citizens, Business and Streets,

AND OTHER USEFUL INFORMATION.

A. B. SPARROW, COMPILER.

The publishers desire to express their thanks to the people of North Andover for the courtesy and aid extended to them in their labor of canvassing for the Directory, and also for the liberal patronage received for their first edition. While efforts have been made to have the Directory correct, patrons will please bear in mind the difficulty of compiling an edition of so large a list of names without an occasional orthographical error; and we trust that all who give the work any attention will look for its merits rather than its defects.

SPARROW & FARNSWORTH,
PUBLISHERS,
SHIRLEY VILLAGE, MASS.

MRS. ELLEN MAHONEY,
—DEALER IN—
Dry and Fancy Goods,
GROCERIES,
BREAD, CAKE AND PASTRY,
Confectionery, &c.

35 East Water Street, North Andover.

J. G. BROWN,
—DEALER IN—
Dry and Fancy Goods,
Hosiery, Underwear, &c.
—ALSO—
A full line of Men's, Women's and Children's
BOOTS, SHOES AND RUBBERS.
Agents for RHODES & MOULTON STEAM LAUNDRY.
Water Street, North Andover.

FRANK M. GREENWOOD,

—DEALER IN—

PURE COCHECIWICK LAKE ICE

Families and Stores Supplied.

Residence, Pond Street, North Andover.

CONTENTS.

Abbreviations,	119
Business Directory,	156
Churches,	107
County Officers,	19
Fire Department,	117
Index to Advertisers,	166
Index to Lawrence Patrons,	EE
Lodges and Societies,	109
Population of Massachusetts, 1890,	167
Post Offices,	115
Postal Rates,	21
Resident Directory,	119
Schools and Teachers,	113
Street Directory,	105
Town Officers,	111

T. A. HOLT & CO.,
―――DEALERS IN―――
DRY GOODS, GROCERIES, HAY, STRAW,
Agricultural Implements, Best Grades of Flour,

And everything usually found in a first-class general store.

Phillips Square,   *North Andover.*

EDMUND S. COLBY.

Insurance. - -

Lowest Rates, Strongest Companies, and Prompt Settlements.

Real Estate - -

Bought and Sold.

LOANS and MORTGAGES NEGOTIATED.

P. O. Address, North Andover Depot.

Office and Residence, Middlesex Street, corner of Dudley.

MISS JULIA C. FLEMING,

Ladies' - Fine - Dressmaking.

LININGS AND TRIMMINGS FURNISHED IF DESIRED.

All orders receive my personal attention.

MAIN STREET, CORNER OF SUTTON,
North Andover.

JOHN L. DOWNING,

✦ Teacher of ✦

Violin, Cornet and Mandolin.

PIANOS TUNED AND REPAIRED.

Residence, High Street, North Andover Depot.

STREETS, AVENUES, ETC.

Andover, from Unitarian church, Center District, to Andover, via estate of Abiel Wilson.
Andover Road, from Boston road, Farnham District, to Andover.
Ashland, from Sutton at railroad station to River View.
Barker, from Sutton to Stevens.
Belmont, off Hodges.
Berry, from Salem Turnpike to Salem Turnpike, via Ingalls crossing.
Beverly, from Suffolk to Middlesex.
Boston Road, from Turnpike, Farnham District, to town line.
Brown's Court, off Water near Engine House.
Chestnut, from Andover, Center District, to Turnpike.
Church, from Main to Water.
Clarendon, from Pleasant to junction of Water and East Water.
Court, from Prospect near cemetery to junction of Pleasant and Osgood.
Cross, from Elm to Church.
Davis, from Main near residence of Patrick Ryan to Pleasant
Dudley, from Maple avenue to Middlesex.
East Water (New Jerusalem), from junction of Clarendon and Water, eastward.
Elm, from Main opp. Greene to junction High and Prescott.
Essex, from the common, Center District, via Boxford road.
Ferry, from River View to the river.
First, from Main to Maple avenue junction Railroad street.
Foster, from Salem, Kimball District, to Pond school house.
Greene, from Shawsheen river to Elm.
High, from Sutton to Water.
Hodges, from Sargent to May.
Johnson, from the common, Center District, to Turnpike, Farnham District school house.
Lawrence, from Shawsheen river, across Railroad street, to North Andover Center.
Lowell Road, from Center District to town line.
Main, from Osgood near town hall, via M. E. church, across B. & M. R. R.

Maple Avenue, from Railroad street, across Second, to Third.
Marblehead, from Sutton to Middlesex.
May, off Hodges.
Merrimac, from Water to Main, opposite Third.
Middlesex, from Lawrence, across Railroad street, to Greene.
Milk, from Johnson to Chestnut.
Osgood, from Andover, across Pleasant, to Great pond.
Pelham, off Middlesex near Lawrence.
Perry, off Lawrence near the river to Pelham.
Phillips Court, off Osgood near Pleasant.
Pond, from Osgood, Pond District, eastward, by Great pond.
Poor's Lane, off Greene.
Prescott, from High near railroad to Stevens.
Prospect, from school house, Center District, to Osgood.
Railroad, from Main near Morton, across Middlesex, to Andover line.
River View, off Sutton opposite Main.
Salem, from the common, Center District, via Foster.
Sargent, off Railroad near Main.
Sargent Court, from Main to Hodges.
School, off Main near Second.
Second, from Main near Keniston block, across Maple avenue, to Railroad avenue.
Stevens, from Unitarian church, Center District, across Pleasant, via residence of M. T. Stevens.
Stonington, from Maple avenue to Middlesex.
Suffolk, from Marblehead to Beverly near the railroad.
Sutton, from Shawsheen bridge to junction of Barker and High.
Third, from Main near Merrimac to Middlesex.
Union, off Railroad opposite Second to Shawsheen river.
Water, from Main near M. E. church to junction of Clarendon and East Water.
White Row, off Osgood, Stevens mill.

GEORGE REXTROW,
Painter & Paper-Hanger.

ALL KINDS OF

KALSOMINING, GRAINING, WHITENING,

Glazing, Etc.

All orders by mail receive prompt attention.

Residence, Church Street, North Andover.

CHURCHES.

FIRST METHODIST EPISCOPAL CHURCH.

Corner Main and Water streets.
PASTOR.—Rev. Henry Matthews.
TRUSTEES.—James Standring, Henry Keniston, Charles Morton, J. E. Brown, E. S. Edmunds, J. M. Towne, D. H. Meserve, J. W. Haigh.
TREASURER.—E. S. Edmunds.
BOARD OF STEWARDS.—J. M. Towne, John Pollard, Mrs. Alice Pollard, D. H. Meserve, Mrs. E. S. Edmunds, J. G. Brown, C. W. Dillon, A. M. Markey, F. W. Abbott, A. W. Brainard.
SUNDAY SCHOOL.—Superintendent, Alba M. Markey; assistant superintendent, E. S. Edmunds; secretary, Henry Webster; treasurer, C. W. Dillon.
HOURS OF SERVICE.—Sunday, preaching at 10.30 a. m. and 6.30 p. m.; Sunday school, 12 m.; Junior Epworth League, 3 p. m.; Epworth League, 5.45 p. m. Thursday evening, prayer meeting at 7.30.
LADIES' SOCIAL CIRCLE.—President, Mrs. J. Pollard.
EPWORTH LEAGUE.—President, Miss Rachel Matthews.
JUNIOR EPWORTH LEAGUE.—Superintendent, Miss Rachel Matthews.

ST. PAUL'S EPISCOPAL CHURCH.

Main street.
Founded in 1880. The present church building was built and consecrated May 17, 1882. First rector, Rev. Augustine H. Amory, followed by Rev. Robert B. Parks and Rev. George Walker.
OFFICERS.—Vestrymen, William J. Dale, J. D. W. French, Joseph Tempest, Solomon Watson, John Wrigerley, Alex. Toothaker, A. Kershaw; clerk of vestry, Jonas Eastwood; treasurer, C. H. Robinson.
SEXTON.—Joseph Midwood.
ORGANIST.—Richard Redman.
Pulpit supplied at present.

SERVICES.—Sunday, 10.30 a. m. and 7 p. m.; Sunday school after morning service; Holy Communion first Sunday in the month. Ladies' Friendly Society meets Thursday evening at Parish rooms. Ladies' Sewing Society meets Tuesday afternoon at Parish rooms.

NORTH PARISH CHURCH (Unitarian).

North Andover Center.
PASTOR.—Rev. Charles Noyes.
PARISH COMMITTEE.—Nathaniel Stevens, Charles F. Johnson, Edward Adams, Mrs. H. N. Stevens, Mrs. Ralph Blake.
TREASURER.—M. T. Stevens.
CLERK.—S. D. Stevens.
SUNDAY SCHOOL—Superintendent, Rev. Charles Noyes.
SERVICES.—Sunday, preaching at 10.30 a. m.; Sunday school, 12 m.

TRINITARIAN CONGREGATIONAL CHURCH.

Elm street.
DEACONS.—J. H. Stone, George E. Hathorn, J. S. Sanborn, C. E. Stillings.
CLERK.—N. P. Frye.
TREASURER.—J. H. Stone.
SUNDAY SCHOOL.—Superintendent, D. W. Carney.
SERVICES.—Sunday, preaching at 10.30; Sunday school, 12 to 1.

EDWARD ADAMS,
Contractor for Road and Bridge Building,
TEAMING, JOBBING, &C.

ICE Supplied in any quantities to stores and families.
Office, Mill Street, North Andover.

BLACKSMITH WORK of all kinds.
HORSE SHOEING and Carriage Work.
SHOP, NORTH ANDOVER CENTER.

LODGES AND SOCIETIES.

A. F. & A. M.
COCHICHEWICK LODGE.

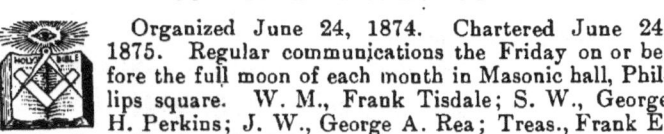
Organized June 24, 1874. Chartered June 24, 1875. Regular communications the Friday on or before the full moon of each month in Masonic hall, Phillips square. W. M., Frank Tisdale; S. W., George H. Perkins; J. W., George A. Rea; Treas., Frank E. Weil; Sec., Charles F. Johnson; Chap., Joseph S. Sanborn; Mar.. George L. Burnham; S. D., Frank A. Warren; J. D., Samuel D. Berry; S. S., Nathan Foster; J. S., Artemas V. Chalk; I. S., William E. Ayers; Organist, Frank D. Foster; Tyler, Frederick P. Hannaford; Relief Committee, Oliver R. Gile, George I. Smith, S. William Ingalls. Secretary's address, P. O. Box 34.

I. O. O. F.
WAUWINET LODGE, No. 111.

Meets Wednesday evenings at 7.45 o'clock in Odd Fellows' hall, Main street. N. G., John B. Lewis; V. G., C. W. Reynolds; Sec., T. P. Wentworth; Treas., George Rextrow; Warden, A. L. Fernandes; Con., John Somerville, Jr.; O. G., J. L. Leighton; I. G., Charles Clark; R. S. N. G., William Halliday, Jr.; L. S. N. G., H. B. Foster; R. S. V. G., F. E. Weil; L. S. V. G., L. C. Wentworth; R. S. S., B. A. Cole; L. S. S., W. G. Stone; Chap., R. W. Walker.

U. O. P. F.
BRADSTREET COLONY, No. 126.

Meets the first and third Tuesday evenings of each month at 8 p. m., in Odd Fellows' hall, Main street, North Andover. The officers are as follows: Gov., A. W. Brainerd; Lieut. Gov., Miss Julia M. Robinson; Sec., E. L. Perley; Collector, A. B. Bixby;

Treas., G. W. Morgan; Chap., Miss Emma F. Trulan; Sergt.-at-Arms, A. V. Chalk; Dept. Sergt.-at-Arms, Miss Mary H. Stone; S. I. G., J. M. Craig; S. O. G., M. Phelan.

I. O. G. T.
WYNONA LODGE, No. 295.

Meets Monday evening in Odd Fellows' hall. C. T., Eugene D. Tufts; V. T., Annie Sutcliffe; Treas., Frank W. Frisbee; Chaplain, Rev. H. Matthews; Sec., Charles W. Hixman; F. S., W. A. Frost; P. C. T., A. V. Chalk; M., Fred A. Carr; G., W. G. Ayers; S., William Drew; Supt. Juvenile Temple, Annie Sutcliffe.

JOHN F. SANBORN,
DOMESTIC ✲ BAKER.

Hot Bread and Rolls Fresh Every Morning.

CAKE, PASTRY, ETC., FRESH EVERY DAY.

Hot Brown Bread Every Saturday Evening.

Send in your orders to the HOME BAKERY,

Stonington Street,   *North Andover.*

EDGAR R. TUCKER,
———PROPRIETOR———
ROSE MEADOW FARM.
———DEALER IN———
PURE MILK.

Families supplied daily.   Send in your orders.

RESIDENCE, ESSEX STREET, NORTH ANDOVER.

TOWN OFFICERS.

SELECTMEN.—Edward W. Greene, Harry W. Clark, Patrick P. Daw.
TOWN CLERK.—James W. Leitch.
TOWN TREASURER.—George H. Perkins.
AUDITOR.—Edwin L. Perley.
COLLECTOR OF TAXES.—Edmund S. Colby.
CLERK OF SELECTMEN.—Harry W. Clark.
ASSESSORS.—The Selectmen.
OVERSEERS OF THE POOR.—The Selectmen.
SUPERINTENDENT OF THE ALMSHOUSE.—Albert Burnham.
CONSTABLES.—Artemas V. Chalk, George I. Smith, George L. Harris, Fred L. Sargent, William J. Toohey.
CHIEF OF POLICE.—Enos S. Robinson.
SURVEYOR AND MEASURER OF LUMBER.—L. S. Perley.
ROAD COMMISSIONERS.—Bradford C. Smith, A. P. Cheeney, James C. Poor.
BOARD OF REGISTRATION.—Calvin Rea, J. W. Leitch, Michael E. Bolton, Alfred L. Fernandes.
TOWN PHYSICIAN.—Dr. F. E. Weil.
BOARD OF HEALTH.—C. P. Morrill, Chairman.
For County Officers, see Andover Directory.

PUBLIC LIBRARY AND READING ROOM.

Odd Fellows' building, Main street. The library contains about 7,100 volumes and is open for the delivery of books Wednesday and Saturday afternoon from 3 to 5 o'clock. The reading room is open every evening from 7 to 9, except legal holidays. Trustees, Dr. Frank E. Weil, J. A. Ellison, Alfred L. Smith.

C. L. FARNSWORTH,

CONCRETE PAVER

—AND—

Gravel Roofer.

Walks, Driveways,

ETC,

CONCRETED BY SKILLED WORKMEN.

ALL WORK GUARANTEED.

Correspondence Solicited.

ADDRESS, - - P. O. BOX 478,

AYER, MASS.

PUBLIC SCHOOLS.

SCHOOL COMMITTEE.—Dr. Charles P. Morrill, Chairman; Miss Mary G. Carleton, Secretary; Dr. Frank E. Weil.

TEACHERS.

HIGH SCHOOL. CENTER DISTRICT.—James C. Flagg, Principal; Miss Annie L. Sargent, Assistant.

MERRIMACK, No. 1.—A. L. Smith, Principal; Miss Laura M. Dunsmoor, Assistant.

MERRIMACK, No. 2.—Miss Hannah C. Carleton.
MERRIMACK, No. 3.—Miss Mary E. Quealey.
MERRIMACK, No. 4.—Miss Helen C. Sargent.
MERRIMACK, No. 5.—Miss Laura A. Bailey.
MERRIMACK, No. 6.—Miss Annie E. Sanborn.
MERRIMACK, No. 7.—Miss Annie M. Osgood.
MERRIMACK, No. 8.—Miss Jean U. Piddington.
UNION No. 1.—Miss Estelle S. Rodgers.
UNION No. 2.—Miss Helen E. Roach.
BRADSTREET No. 1.—Miss Anna M. Tucker.
BRADSTREET No. 2.—Miss Henrietta Hatch.
CENTER, No. 1.—Miss Ella A. Small.
CENTER, No. 2.—Miss Mary B. Sproul.
FARNHAM DISTRICT.—Miss Maud Randall.
KIMBALL DISTRICT.—Miss B. Letitia Wilcox.
POND DISTRICT.—Miss Margaret P. Hubbard.
RIVER DISTRICT.—Miss Hattie M. Ellis.
MUSIC.—Edward Butterworth.
DRAWING.—Miss Harriet D. Coudon.

JAMES W. LEITCH,
—DEALER IN—
STOVES, ✻ RANGES,

OIL STOVES
—AND—
KITCHEN GOODS,
Copper and Granite Ware,
Etc. Agent for .
MAGEE RANGES.

Also, all kinds of Contract Work, Plumbing, Repairing, etc.,
DONE BY SKILLED WORKMEN.

Store, Water Street, under Merrimack Hall, North Andover.

P. O. Address, North Andover Depot.

JOHN WILCOX,

Manufacturer of
ALL KINDS OF
Heavy Wagons
—AND—
CARTS.

HORSE SHOEING
OUR SPECIALTY.

Special attention given Difficult Shoeing.

BLACKSMITH WORK
OF ALL KINDS.

Andover Street,   North Andover.

POSTOFFICES.

NORTH ANDOVER POST-OFFICE.

Isaac F. Osgood, Postmaster; Mrs. L. M. Osgood, Assistant Postmaster; Clerk, A. S. Ingalls.

Mails arrive from South and West at 9 a. m., 2 and 5.10 p. m.; from Newburyport, 10.30 a. m. Mails close for South and West at 9 and 10.30 a. m., 5 p. m.; for Newburyport, 2 p. m.

NORTH ANDOVER STATION.

Charles A. Pilling, Postmaster.

Mails arrive from Boston, 7.15 and 8.37 a. m., 1.05 and 4.49 p. m.; from North Andover, 9.30 and 11 a. m., 5.30 p. m.; from Portland, 12.05 and 6.56 p. m.; from Lawrence, 1.30 p. m. Mails close for the East, 8.37 a. m., 4.49 p. m.; for Boston, 10.20 a. m., 12.04 and 6.56 p. m.; Lawrence and North, 11 a. m.; North Andover, 8.50 a. m., 1.30 and 5 p. m.; for Salem, 1.07 p. m.

For Postage Rates, see page 21.

EDWARD COOPER,
—DEALER IN—

Choice Family
GROCERIES,
Home-Made Bread,
Select Brands Flour,
ALSO,
CORN, MEAL,
Cigars, Tobacco, Etc.

41 MAIN STREET,   *NORTH ANDOVER.*

J. JACOBS,
—DEALER IN—
COAL and LUMBER.

Constantly in stock, all the best qualities of

Anthracite and Cumberland Coal.
—ALSO,—

Spruce and Pine Lumber,
Shingles, Lath, Clapboards,
Etc.

OFFICE AND YARD,
MAIN STREET, near SUTTON.

MRS. ELLEN T. MORRISSEY,
—PROPRIETOR—

MAIN STREET
Dining Rooms.

Board by the day or week,
with or without rooms,
at reasonable rates.

Confectionery, Cigars,
Etc.

Bread, Cake and Pastry fresh every day.
MAIN STREET, OPP. FIRST, NORTH ANDOVER.

J. W. RICHARDSON,
—DEALER IN—

FINE GROCERIES,
Selected Teas, Coffees and Spices,
BUTTER AND CHEESE
From the best Vermont and New York Dairies.

Choice Syrup and Molasses. Canned Fruit in Variety.

CHOICE BRANDS OF FLOUR,

And a complete assortment of goods usually kept in a first-class grocery store.

Main Street, North Andover.

FIRE DEPARTMENT.

BOARD OF ENGINEERS.—William A. Johnson, Charles H. Shedd, Clerk; George Stone.

EBEN SUTTON STEAMER, No. 1.

Capt., John Burnham; 1st Lieut., Frank A. Coan; Clerk, A. W. Badger; Treas., Martin H. Pulsifer; Engineer, Enos S. Robinson; Asst. Engineer, Horace E. Towne; S. Hoseman, George Rextrow; 1st Pipeman, William R. Johnson; 2d Pipeman, Willard H. Handy; 3d Pipeman, Charles A. Dame; 4th Pipeman, Eli H. Watts; Driver of Steamer, Wellington Davis; Driver of Hose Wagon, George H. Mizen; Hosemen, Daniel W. Sutcliffe Walter G. Stone, Charles B. Smith.

COCHICHEWICK ENGINE COMPANY, No. 2.

Center District. Chief Engineer, William A. Johnson; Assistant, George Stone; Clerk, Charles Shedd; Capt., G. F. Royal; 1st Assistant, Timothy Eagan; 2d Assistant, George H. Wilton; Clerk, John Herbert; 41 call men.

J. E. REYNOLDS & SON,
CIDER MAKERS
—AND DEALERS IN—
CIDER AND VINEGAR.
JOHNSON STREET, FARNHAM DISTRICT,
North Andover.

McDONALD & HANNAFORD,

(Established 1820,)

—MANUFACTURER OF—

COUPE, BUGGY AND DOUBLE HARNESS,

—ALSO,—

CARRIAGE PAINTING

—AND—

TRIMMING.

All Work Warranted.

ORDERS BY MAIL RECEIVE PROMPT ATTENTION.

NORTH ANDOVER, MASS.

A. McDONALD.   F. P. HANNAFORD.

JOHN H. FULLER,

—DEALER IN—

Dry Goods, Groceries, Boots, Shoes and Rubbers,

CHOICE BRANDS OF FLOUR, GRAIN, FEED,

Fertilizers, Garden Produce, AGRICULTURAL IMPLEMENTS, &c.

Elm Street, near Water, North Andover.

North Andover Resident Directory.

ABBREVIATIONS USED.

Av., avenue; bds., boards; c., corner; ct., court; emp., employe; h., house; n., near; opp., opposite; pl., place; r., rear; sq., square; C. D., Center District; F. D., Farnham District; K. D., Kimball District; P. D., Pond District; R. D., River District.

A

ABBOTT FRANCES M. MRS. (Caleb) house Maple av.
" Frank W. clerk J. H. Fuller, house Maple av.
" George W. farmer, house Salem, K. D.
" Lucy, house Judson E. Reynolds
" Lydia J. Mrs. (Asa H.) house High
Adams Charles B. card setter, house High
ADAMS EDWARD, contractor, house Milk, C. D.
" Elizabeth S. Mrs. (John) house Milk
" Mary, Mrs. (Charles) house White Row
Allen Ambrose, laborer, house Johnson, F. D. near schoolhouse
" Joseph F. boards William A. Evans
" Simon P. laborer, house Stevens
" William, house Stevens, C. D.
" William, house Ambrose do.
" William, emp. Davis & Furber, house foot Maple av.
" William, Jr. machinist, boards William do.
Apthorp William A. house Prospect
Anderson David, machinist, boards Thomas P. Wills
" Jane, Mrs. (Christian) house Stevens cor. Pleasant
Armitage Margaret (M. & M. J. Armitage) fancy goods and dressmaking, Main, house Main near First
" Mary J. (M. & M. J. Armitage) house Main near First
Atkins Newell E. farmer, house Turnpike, F. D.

Upon the Purity of Drugs and the reliability of our work we depend. **PERKINS, THE DRUGGIST.**

Averill George L. house Forest
Ayer William E. watchman, house Water corner Church

B

BABB WILLIAM H. house Water
Badger Alphonso W. emp. card clothing room, house High near Water
" Orrin, emp. Davis & Furber, house Maple av.
Badget George, oiler, house 5 Beverly
Bailey Hannah R. teacher, house Osgood near junction Main
" John T. B. farm hand, house Lake View Farm
" Laura A. teacher, house Osgood near junction Main
Baker Austin, emp. Isaac L. Farnham, boards do.
" John T. house Suffolk
Baldwin Eben A. (Davis & Furber) house Elm near Water
" William, house Pleasant
Banks Isaiah, laborer, house Johnson, F. D.
Banford Joseph, laborer, house 32 River View
Bannam Catherine Mrs. (Peter) house John F. do.
" John F. chemist Stevens mill, house Osgood n. Pleasant
Barcroft Henry, emp. Stevens mill, house Pleasant near Stevens
Barden Bradford H. house Sutton
" Fred P. house Sutton
Barker Andrew J. watchman Davis & Furber, house 58 Water
" Charles O. house Bradford
" George L. meat and provisions, house Maple av.
" Horace E. house Andrew J. do.
" Jacob, house Bradford
" John, farmer, house Pond, River District
Barnard Margaret Mrs. (Frank) house Charles Dame
Barrett Patrick, flannel scourer, house Ferry
Barrington Peter, blacksmith, house Union near Marblehead
Bartlett Boyd, house Osgood
Barty William, machinist, house 24 East Water
Barwell Harry, dresser, house Sutton c. Main
Bassett Leon H. fruit canning, house Osgood, R. D.
Bateman Francis A. emp. finishing room, Stevens mill, house White Row
Batson Joshua B. carpenter, house Belmont
Battles Joseph, mfr. of machinery, Lawrence, house Stevens near Prescott
" Joseph P. (Lawrence Machine Co.) house Stevens near Prescott
Bauchman Daniel, iron moulder, house School

For Quality and Price PERKINS' Extract Jamaica Ginger leads them all. **PERKINS, THE DRUGGIST.**

Baxter William R. emp. Davis & Furber, house Pleasant
Bean Peter, blacksmith, house off 59 Water
Bedell John A. machinist, house Second near Main
Bell David, cloth inspector, house White Row
Bencker John A. house Salem, K. D.
Bennett John F. clerk G. L. Barker, house Lawrence
" Joseph J. emp. Sagehomme & Byers, house Sutton
Berrian George W. house Salem, K. D.
Berry Albert Mrs. house Turnpike, F. D.
" Charles Q. teamster, house Marblehead
" Charles A. farmer, house Turnpike, F. D.
" Daniel G. farmer, house Turnpike, near Middleton line
" Herford, student, house Andover, C. D.
" Samuel D. farmer, house Turnpike, F. D.
Bickford Thomas J. overseer Marble Ridge farm, house Essex
Bilodeau Louis, loom fixer, house Lawrence c. Perry
Bisbee Charles F. farmer, house Osgood, R. D.
BISHOP FRANCIS R. clerk T. A. Holt & Co. boards A. N. Holt
Bixby Alonzo, tinsmith, house Pleasant c. Clarendon
" Amos B. machinist, house 12 Pleasant
" Sarah I. bookkeeper, house Amos B. do.
Black Thomas D. house Turnpike
Blake Joseph P. house Andover
" Ralph, farmer, house Andover, C. D.
Blanchard Ann Mrs. (Daniel) house Brown's court
" George W. machinist, house Pleasant near Davis
Blunt Abigail Mrs. house Salem near Marble Ridge station
" Lois A. house Salem near Marble Ridge station
Bode Julius, farmer, house Ingalls crossing
" William J. farmer, house Julius do.
Bodwell Stephen B. farmer, house Osgood, R. D.
" Herbert, motorman, house Sutton near Shawsheen river
Bolton John W. conductor, house foot Belmont
" Michael E. machinist, house 54 East Water
" Sabian, gardener M. T. Stevens, house Stevens
Bonner William W. spinner Stevens mill, house Phillips court
Booth J. W. emp. Sutton's mill, boards Mrs. Kate Kilburn
Brackett James L. clerk Davis & Furber, house Samuel Ligget
Bradley Catherine, house Pleasant near Elm
Brailsford George, gardener, house Marblehead c. Middlesex
" Harry, mule spinner, house Middlesex
" John, gardener, house Marblehead c. Middlesex
Brainerd Albert, second hand, card room, house Albert W. do.
" Albert W. overseer Pacific mills, house Marblehead

If you want Patent Medicines at cut-rate prices, (guaranteed genuine,) go to **PERKINS, the Druggist.**

Brierley Annie Mrs. (Edmond) house Water, 4 Yellow Row
" Benjamin, conductor, house Belmont
" James, carpenter, house Sutton
" James, farmer, house Prescott
" John A. machinist, house Prescott
" Joseph J. machinist, house 19 Beverly
" Rachel Mrs. (Joseph) house 19 Beverly
Briggs Peter, machinist, house Sargent
Broderick Bridget Mrs. (Hugh) house Phillips court n. Pleasant
" Thomas, emp. Stevens mill, house Mrs. Bridget do.
Brodhead James, house Railroad near Second
Brodie John, house Stevens Village
" Peter, house Stevens near Pleasant
" William S. overseer weaving room, Stevens mill, house Stevens near Pleasant
Brooks Allen, dresser, house Railroad c. Union
" William G. house Osgood, in summer
Brown James, machinist, house Pelham
BROWN J. G. dry and fancy goods, boots, shoes and rubbers, Water, house do.
" Nelson, farm hand, house Frederick Cummings
" Robert, emp. Mrs. Henrietta A. Kittredge, boards do.
" Thomas, emp. Davis & Furber, house 65 Water
Bruce Andrew, house Second
" David, blacksmith, house 27 East Water
" Elizabeth Mrs. (Andrew) house Second near Main
" William, blacksmith, house Mrs. Elizabeth do.
" William W. fireman B. & M. R. R. house David do.
Bryant Frank L. teaming and jobbing, house Middlesex
Buckley George, farm hand, house Frederick Cummings
Bucknam Arthur S. house Salem
Burke Michael, farmer, house Milk
" Simeon, machinist, boards Mrs. W. B. Perkins
Burnham Albert P. supt. N. A. almshouse, house Dale, P. D.
" John, iron moulder, house 25 Elm
Burns George M. carpenter, house Johnson, C. D.
Buskirk Benjamin, house Pond
Butterfield Charles A. farmer, h. Salem n. Marble Ridge station
" Charles H. farmer, boards Charles A. do.
Butterworth Edward, instructor in music, h. Main c. Merrimac
" Edward P. machinist, house Mrs. John do.
" George H. machinist, house Mrs. John do.
" John, Mrs. house High near Sutton

If you have a tired feeling after seeing Perkins, the Druggist, on all these pages, buy a bottle of his superior Beef, Wine and Iron.

C

Cain John, house Osgood
Callahan Dennis, emp. Stevens mill, house Pleasant near Stevens
" John, house Stevens Village
" Josephine, house Marblehead
" Mary, house Marblehead
" Patrick, farmer, house Stevens, C. D.
" Thomas, twister, house River View
Cameron John C. carpenter, house Marblehead corner Middlesex
Campbell James F. carpenter, house 7 Beverly
" John H. emp. B. & M. R. R. house Second n. Railroad st.
" Michael F. manufacturer near Shawsheen Bridge, house Ashland opposite railroad station
Carey John, laborer, house Lawrence corner Perry
" Lawrence M. house Greene near Middlesex
Carleton Amos D. house Farnum
" Daniel A. house Summer
" Hannah C. teacher, house Main near Second
" John F. Mrs. house Dale, P. D.
" Mary G. secretary of the board of school committee, house Main near Second
" Susan E. clerk A. Sharpe & Co. Lawrence, house Main near Second
Carney Daniel W. supt. Standard Oil Co. house Second near Maple av.
" John, section hand B. & M. R. R. house Main opp. First
" Hannah, domestic, house George E. Curwen
" Michael, house Osgood
Carpenter Edwin H. carpenter, house 23 East Water
Carr John, section hand Pacific mill, house 10 Beverly
" John V. blacksmith, house High near Sutton
Carroll James, house Railroad
" John, house Railroad near Main
" Joanna, house James F. Murphy
" Thomas, laborer, house Railroad near Main
Carter Annie M. house Mrs. Betsey C. do.
" Betsey C. Mrs. (Thomas P.) house 27 Pleasant
" Ezra A. foreman J. H. Stone, house Middlesex n. Greene
" Fred, house Pond
" Henry, yarn shipper, house 18 Beverly
" Irving, house Water
" John C. carpenter, house Belmont
Casey Maurice J. house Stevens near Salem, C. D.
Cassidy Patrick, dyer, house Railroad corner Middlesex

❋ PERKINS, ❋ THE ❋ DRUGGIST. ❋

Castello Dennis J. contractor and builder, house Union corner Marblehead
" James P. machinist, house 23 Main
" Patrick, laborer, house Water, 13 Yellow Row
Chadwick George G. farmer, house Osgood, R. D.
" J. Gilbert, farmer, house Osgood, R. D.
" Robert, watchmaker and jeweler, house Marblehead cor. Middlesex
" William B. farmer, house High
Chalk Artemas V. painter, house Main junction Water
Chapin Benjamin F. blacksmith and wheelwright, house Main corner Railroad
Charlesworth John R. weaver, boards James Broadhead
Chase Frank W. farmer, house near Pond school
" Parker, blacksmith, house Pleasant
Cheever William J. Capt. house Salem near Marble Ridge station
Chenery James, house Turnpike
Cheney Ariel P. livery stable and variety store Water cor. Elm, house Elm cor. Water
" Clara E. house Ariel P. do.
" George A. emp. B. & M. car shop, house Elm c. Water
Chesley Ervan E. card setter, house 25 East Water
" Laura J. Mrs. (James) house Ervan E. do.
Chickering Arthur P. law student, house William W. do.
" William W. foreman Davis & Furber, house Main c. School
Childs George, house Osgood
" William W. house Osgood
Christenson Hans, melter, house Maple av.
Churbuck Archibald G. office of M. T. Stevens & Sons, house Edwin W. Moody
Church George, blacksmith, house River View near the brook
" Joseph, laborer, house foot Main
" Joseph, laborer, house River View near the brook
Clapperton Ellen Mrs. house James do.
" James, emp. Sutton's mill, house Water, 7 Yellow Row
" Thomas, emp. Sutton's mill, house Water, 8 Yellow Row
Clark Charles L. farmer, house William do.
" Edith M. house John do.
" E. Francis, house Main
" Edward, boards Abiel Wilson
" Fred, house Johnson
" F. C. house Main
" George B. house William do.
" Harry W. chemist, house High near Sutton

Hair, Tooth, Nail and Shaving Brushes at all prices. PERKINS, the Druggist.

Clark Hiram F. wood worker Milk, house do.
" John, carpenter, house off 6 Water
" John Peters, farmer, house Chestnut, C. D.
" William C. farmer, house Berry near Middleton line
Clarkin Peter, wool sorter, boards John Wilton
Clements William J. coachman George G. Davis, house Davis
Coan Frank A. emp. card clothing room, Davis & Furber, house First
Cogswell Mary L. house near Marble Ridge station
" Susan L. Mrs. (William A.) house near Marble Ridge station

COLBY EDMUND S. insurance and real estate, Middlesex, house do.

Cole Edmund, house Pleasant
" John, house Pleasant
Coleman Delia, domestic, house George E. Curwen
" Fred W. draughtsman, house Mrs. Isabel do.
" Henry N. machinist, house Pleasant near Davis
" Isabel Mrs. (John J.) house Pleasant near Davis
" Ralph T. machinist, house Pleasant near Davis
Collier William, weaver, house Railroad near Second
Collina William, shoe repairer Water, house do.
Collins Dennis F. blacksmith, house Church near Water
" John J. machinist, boards Patrick P. do.
" Patrick P. laborer, house Railroad corner Union
Connelly John, flagman B. & M. R. R. house Main opp. school house
" Michael, clerk J. R. Simpson, Lawrence, house John do.
" Thomas M. house Parker
Connors Daniel, house Water
" Mary, weaver, house Mrs. Jane Curtin
Conway Michael, house Summer

COOPER EDWARD, groceries, flour, etc. 41 Main, house do.

Coppinger Thomas, house 30 East Water
Corchrane Russell, house Osgood
Corsey Thomas, house Henry B. Engley
Costello Edward, house Water
" Edward A. house Ashland
" Eliza, domestic, house Joseph H. Stone
" Eliza C. Mrs. (John) house Osgood near Andover
" Ellen Mrs. (Michael) house Ashland near railroad station
" Oliver, laborer, house Railroad
" Oliver T. house Ashland
Cothill Isaac, machinist, boards Mrs. W. B. Perkins

PERKINS, the Druggist, has recommendations from the leading physicians.

Coughlin John J. laborer, house Mrs. Mary do.
" Kate Mrs. (James) house First
" Mary Mrs. (James) house Second near Railroad st.
" Nellie D. dressmaker, house Mrs. Mary do.
Coyne John P. wool carder, house 17 East Water
Craig James M. janitor of school house, house Main opp. First
" William H. house 26 River View
Crockett John C. carpenter, house Main near Third
" Mary Mrs. house Sutton near Sagehomme & Byers' mill
" Robert, weaver, boards Mrs. Mary do.
" Robertina Mrs. (Robert) house Second c. Railroad
Cronin John, watchman North Andover mill, house Water, 11 Yellow Row
Cronley Daniel, section hand B. & M. R. R. house Main near railroad crossing
" Daniel, Jr. section hand B. & M. R. R. house Daniel do.
" John A. moulder, house Daniel do.
" Mary Mrs. (Edward) house Maple av.
" Martha, house Daniel do.
Crowther John, machinist, house Pleasant near Davis
" James W. emp. Stevens mill, house John
Cummings Frederick, foreman Russell's farm, house Osgood near Pleasant
Cunningham William, weaver, house off Main rear old drug store
Curley Patrick H. machinist, house 3 Beverly
Curwen George E. leather business Boston, house Stevens
Currier Aaron A. contractor and builder, house Prescott
" Arthur P. (A. P. Currier & Co.) grocer Water, house Pleasant corner Clarendon
Curtin Dennis, emp. Sutton mill, house Sutton
" Fannie, boards Patrick McEvoy
" Jane Mrs. (John) house Water near engine house
" John, moulder, house 46 East Water
" Mary, boards Mrs. Ellen Donovan
" William, emp. Sutton mill, house Dennis do.

D

Dale William J. Dr. house Dale
" William J. Jr. railroad commissioner, h. William J. do.
Daley John, laborer, house Ferry
Dalton Mary, house Mrs. Catherine Harper
Dame Charles A. machinist, house Water near engine house
Damren William H. house Lawrence

Strictly pure articles, and exactly as represented, is the reputation of **PERKINS, THE DRUGGIST.**

Danahey Delia, house Mrs. Hannah McCarthy
" Frank, moulder, boards Mrs. Hannah McCarthy
Danforth Llewellyn, machinist, boards 68 Water
Davis Frank, farmer, house Osgood near Andover
" George E. house Bradford
" George G. (Davis & Furber) house Main near Greene
" George W. house Main
" Nancy Mrs. (John) house 68 Water
" Wellington, driver Eben Sutton Steamer, No. 1, boards 68 Water
Davitt John, emp. Stevens mill, house off Prospect, C. D.
Daw Mary Mrs. (Thomas) house William J. Donovan
" Patrick P. contractor and builder, house Second n. Main
Deadier James, watchman Stevens mill, house White Row
Dearmon John, farm hand, house Charles D. Frost
Deming Jane Mrs. house Cross
Demangel Henry, boards Joseph J. Bennett
Dewhint William, house River
Dewhurst John, cloth inspector, house Pelham
" John D. cloth inspector, Washington mills, house Perry
Dodge George E. station agent, house Union near Railroad
Dick Violet Mrs. (Peter) house Sutton near railroad station
Dickey George I. card setter, house 14 Pleasant
Diggle Samuel, blacksmith, house Clarendon c. Water
Dill Frederick, house Stevens
Dillon Patrick, emp. Davis & Furber, house Osgood n. town hall
" William C. house Main
Doherty Edward B. milkman, house Patrick do.
" Frank, emp. Sutton mill, house Water, 4 Yellow Row
" Patrick, milkman, house First
Donnelly John J. watchman, house 33 River View
" —— Mrs. house White Row
Donovan Andy, emp. Charles Wilcox, boards do.
" Charles J. house Osgood
" Daniel J. laborer, house Ellis block, Main
" Dennis E. house Second
" Ellen Mrs. (John) house Ellis block, Main
" Hannah, house Mrs. Ellen do.
" Johanna Mrs. house Sargent
" John J. house Second
" Michael W. house Second
" Patrick, laborer, house Maple avenue
" Patrick, emp. Charles Wilcox, boards do.
" Timothy J. moulder, house Ashland opp. railroad station
" William J. machinist, house Cross

All Patent Medicines sold at bottom prices, by Perkins, the Druggist.

Dooley James J. house Main
" John A. machinist, house Thomas do.
" Michael J. house Thomas do.
" Thomas, laborer, house Union c. Railroad
" Thomas F. moulder, house Thomas do.
Doran Patrick, emp. B. & M. R. R. house Hodges
Dore William, card setter, house 5 Pleasant
Dow James A. house Pleasant
" Moses A. machinist, house 7 Pleasant
Downes William P. coachman William Hall, Jr. house Davis
Downing Eben B. card setter, house Elm near Pleasant
" Horace F. house Second
Downing John J. house High
DOWNING JOHN L. teacher violin, cornet and mandolin, house Leverett H. do.
" Leverett H. machinist, house High near Water
" Samuel, emp. Davis & Furber, house 19 Church
Drew Frank H. blacksmith, house 4 Pleasant
" Thomas H. emp. Davis & Furber, house Davis
Driscoll John A. (Driscoll and O'Brien) mason and builder, house Salem Turnpike
" Katie F. house Joseph Reagan
" Mary J. house Joseph Reagan
" Michael, fireman Sutton mill, h. Water, 6 Yellow Row
" Thomas, emp. Davis & Furber, h. Water, 2 Yellow Row
" William, laborer, boards Mrs. Ellen Mahoney
Driver James, overseer wool scouring, Stevens mill, house Osgood near Pleasant
Dryden William F. dresser, house foot River View
Duffy John, laborer, house Sutton near railroad station
Dufrens Joseph, carpenter, house 29 East Water
Dunbar Martin W. machinist, house 7 Water
Duncan John, house Tucker
" Robert, house Pleasant
Dunn James, house Osgood
" William, machinist, boards Thomas P. Wills
Dunnils George W. mason and builder, house off Main
Duprey Frank I. operative Davis & Furber, house School
Dwyer Mary, house Thomas F. Morrissey

E

Eagan Michael, emp. Stevens mill, house White Row
" Timothy, house Michael do.
Eastwood Jonas, machinist, house 26 East Water

LIQUIDONIA, FOR CHAPPED HANDS, is of more value for the money

Eaton Frank W. machinist, house Second near Main
" Lucy J. Mrs. (Joseph) house Frank W. do.
Edmunds Edward S. foreman M. T. Stevens' farm, house Stevens c. Osgood
Elliot John, house Johnson
" Mary A. house Robert
" Robert, boss finisher, Sutton mill, house Sutton near Sutton mill

ELLIS ARNO P. blacksmith and wheelwright, house Main opp. Railroad
" Hattie, teacher, house Horatio do.
" Horatio B. house Sutton
" Joseph W. blacksmith, house A. P. do.
" Leander S. farmer, house Essex, P. D.
" William, house Marblehead near Railroad
Ellison J. Albert, machinist, house Stonington
Elvey Annie, house Mrs. Mary A. do.
" Mary A. Mrs. (Henry) house 6 Pleasant
Emery George A. teamster Davis & Furber, house 12 Water
Emmett John, emp. Pacific mill, house 31 Beverly
" Joseph W. machinist, house 31 Beverly
Ernst John E. weaver, house 14 Beverly
Estes Frank E. house Stevens Village
Eugley Henry B. painter, h. Main opp. Bradstreet school house
Evans Charles S. teamster, house Osgood near Andover
" Samuel, boards William A. do.
" William A. house Salem c. Stevens, C. D.
" William E. house Salem

F

FARMER ALFRED H. house Mrs. Hannah J. do.
" Hannah J. Mrs. (Alfred) house Main c. Railroad
Farnham Arthur, farmer, house Seth do.
" Charles H. farmer, house Andover near Lowell road
" Holt, house off Turnpike, F. D.
" Isaac L. farmer, house Andover near Lowell road
" Jacob L. farmer, house Turnpike, F. D.
" John I. farmer, house Johnson, C. D.
" Martha, house John I. do.
" Seth T. farmer, house Turnpike, F. D.
Farnum Benjamin H. house Farnum
" Benjamin W. house Farnum
" Jacob L. house Turnpike

Than any other article of its kind. 25 cents a bottle, at **PERKINS', the Druggist.**

Farrell James, farmer, house White Row
Farris Willard, gardener, house M. T. Stevens place
" William, second gardener M. T. Stevens, house Church near Water
Faulkner George H. house Water
Felker Herbert K. emp. electric railway, boards Frank E. Oxton
Fenton Thomas, machinist, house Water c. Church
Fernandes Alfred L. machinist, house High
Fernandez Daniel L. house Pleasant c. Davis
Fernald Waldina L. house Pleasant
" William M. emp. Davis & Furber, house 2 Pleasant
Ferson Charles A. moulder, house 24 Pleasant
" Elmer, house Pleasant
Field Herbert W. bank teller Essex Savings Bank, Lawrence. house Main near Elm
" Henry P. house Osgood
Fielding Albert, house Water, 17 Yellow Row
" Hattie, house Water, 17 Yellow Row
" Joseph, spinner, house Water, 9 Yellow Row
" John, house Main
Finn John T. machinist, boards Mrs. Margaret Winning
" Thomas, second hand Stevens mill, house off Pleasant, Stevens Village
Finnegan James J. groceries and provisions, house Sutton
Fish Arthur E. house Salem
" Edith S. stenographer, house John C. do.
" Isaac. house Foster, K. D.
" Jennie P. house John C. do.
" John C. farmer, house off Andover, C. D.
" Jonathan H. house Depot, C. D.
" Orrin M. machinist, house John C. do.
" Samuel A. house Isaac do.
Fisher Edwin, farmer, house Turnpike, F. D.
" James, house Water
Fitzgerald James, coachman, house George E. Curwen
Flagg James C. principal high school, boards A. N. Holt
Flannigan John, emp. Stevens mill, house Pleasant near Stevens
Fleming David A. moulder, boards Mrs. Ellen do.
" Ellen Mrs. (David) house River View
FLEMING JULIA C. dressmaker, house Main c. Sutton

Fling Warren B. farm hand, house Edgar R. Tucker
Flynn Burton G. house 6 Water
" Charles, house Church

DR. BIGELOW'S GREAT ENGLISH COUGH CURE is the

Flynn Elmer, machinist, house White Row
" Irving, emp. Stevens mill, house White Row
" Owen, house William W. Bonner
" Sarah Mrs. (Owen) house White Row
Fogarty John, carpenter, boards Mrs. Hannah McCarthy
Foran Patrick, emp. B. & M. R. R. boards Patrick Doran
Ford John, emp. J. H. D. Smith, boards do.
Foss Eugene P. farmer, house Essex, P. D.
" Gilman P. farmer, house Essex, P. D.
Fossett Joseph, farmer, house Salem, K. D.
Foster Albert D. carpenter, house High
" Dane, painter, house Bradford, P. D.
" Ellen E. Mrs. (Charles S.) house Foster, K. D.
" Etta, house Phineas do.
" Frank D. house Third
" Herbert L. farmer, house Mrs. Ellen E. do.
" Horace B. machinist, house Phineas do.
" J. Frank, farmer, house Essex, P. D.
" Nathan, farmer, house Dale, P. D.
" Natt, farmer, house Andover
" Orrin N. farmer, house Foster, K. D.
" Phineas, house High
" Sarah Mrs. (John) house Stevens near Salem
" Sarah A. Mrs. (John P.) house J. Frank do.
" Sarah P. house J. Frank do.
Fountain Joseph W. machinist, house 19 East Water
Fox Walter, laborer, boards David H. Jackson
France Ellen Mrs. (Richard) house James Brierly
French J. D. W. office 160 State street, Boston, h. Osgood, R. D.
Frisbee Frank W. tinsmith, house Third near Main
" Ida E. house Frank W. do.
Frost Charles D. farmer, house Pond opp. Lake View farm
" William, machinist, house 17 Pleasant
" William A. student, house William do.
Frye Newton P. counsellor at law, P. O. building, Lawrence, house 23 Elm
Fuller Abijah P. farmer, house Salem, K. D.
" Carrie R. dressmaker, boards Abijah P. do.
" Edward A. farmer, boards Abijah P. do.
" Ernest P. student, boards Abijah P. do.
" George S. student, boards Abijah P. do.
FULLER J. H. dry goods and groceries, Elm, house do.
Furber S. Henry, machinist, house Elm opp. Pleasant

Best Remedy on the market. 25 Cents, at **PERKINS', the Druggist.**

G

GAFFNEY SYLVESTER, machinist, boards Mrs. Ellen T. Morrissey
Gage Nathaniel, house Bradford
Galvin Johanna, domestic, house Thomas P. Wills
Gamble George, teamster, house Lake View farm
Garbutt William, machinist, house Water near engine house
Garner Edward, emp. Davis & Furber, house First
Garside Stephen, spinner, house Phillips court near Pleasant
Garvin Edward, laborer, house Andover, Center District
" Joseph, moulder, boards Edward do.
Geaney William H. gardener, house opp. 5 Pleasant
Gemmell William, foreman W. M. Salisbury, house near Lake View farm
" William, Jr. milkman, house near Lake View farm
Gile Arthur O. machinist, house Main near Merrimac
" Frank S. machinist, house First
" Oliver R. machinist, house High
" William, machinist, house 11 East Water
Gill John G. M. farm hand, boards W. H. Hayes
Gillen Hugh, emp. Stevens mill, house First
Gillespie John, second hand card room Sutton mill, h. Patrick do.
" Patrick, spinner, house Sutton near Sutton mill
Gillooly Patrick, laborer, house Suffolk corner Beverly
Gilman Thomas K. leather dealer 155 Federal, Boston, house Pleasant corner Davis
Glennie Alfred J. soap maker, boards John do.
" Charles D. house Bradford
" James, farmer, house Dale, P. D.
" James Jr. house Bradford
" John, soap mfr. house Lawrence (air line road)
Godfrey Alice J. house Joseph H. Stone
" Oscar M. clerk Davis & Furber, house High
Goff Samuel, spinner, house Sutton
" William, spinner, house 30 River View
Golden Jerry, iron moulder, house 38 East Water
Goodbody William, house Main
Goodhue Frank H. farmer, house Moses do.
" George H. farmer, house Johnson, F. D.
" Hiram, house Turnpike, F. D.
" Levi, farmer, house George H. do.
" Moses, farmer, house Boston road, F. D.
Gordon Myra G. house Joseph H. Stone
Gould Eliza A. Mrs. (Albert) house Milk

Physicians' Prescriptions and all Medicinal Compounds

Gould Frank M. farmer, boards Mrs. Lucy F. do.
" George, painter and paper hanger, house Osgood near junc. Main
" Lucy F. Mrs. (Charles G.) house Andover, C. D.
Graham Alexander B. wool sorter, house 16 Beverly
Gray Benjamin O. house Stiles
" Caroline Mrs. (Henry) house Boston road, F. D.
" Osgood, farmer, house Andover road, F. D.
Green David H. spinner, house Perry c. Pelham
Greene Annie M. house Edward W. do.
" Edward, farmer, house Poor's lane
" Edward W. real estate, house Greene
Greenleaf Rosanna E. Mrs. (George L.) house John G. Brown
Greenwood B. Lewis, house Beverly
GREENWOOD FRANK M. ice, house Pond, R. D.
" Henry, moulder, house off 60 Water
" Joseph, machinist, house Railroad corner Sargent
" Samuel M. house Pond
" Sarah Mrs. (Samuel) house Frank M. do.
Griffin Thomas, farm hand, house Miss Catherine Johnson
Groesback Edson, painter, house 10 Pleasant
Grogan Annie A. dressmaker, house William do.
" Daniel J. carpenter, house William do.
" Edward F. carpenter, house William do.
" John P. machinist, house William do.
" William, iron moulder, house Second near Main
" William T. iron moulder, house William do.
Grozelier Sarah P. Mrs. (Leopold) house Chestnut, C. D.
Guilmette Catherine Mrs. house Frank I. Duprey

H

HAGGERTY CORNELIUS, laborer, boards Mrs. Ellen Mahoney
" Michael, fireman E. P. station, h. Ellis block, Main
Haigh William, tinsmith, house Second near Main
Hainsworth Benjamin, machinist, house Samuel do.
" Samuel P. machinist, house Marblehead
" William, house Samuel do.
Hall Edward L. emp. Stevens mill, boards John Wilton
" George A. machinist, house Maple av.
" Isaac, gardener, house Pleasant near Stevens
" Lydia A. Mrs. (Charles W.) house Maple av.
" W. A. house Chestnut near the reservoir
" William A. jr. house Chestnut, C. D.

Prepared with care and accuracy. Perkins, the Druggist.

Halliday William, house Water
" William, Jr. paymaster at Davis & Furber, house Water
Halpin John, moulder, boards Mrs. Hannah McCarthy
Halsby William, house Bradford
Hamlin Samuel, clerk A. P. Currier, h. Water n. engine house
Hammond Alfred, carpenter, house Middlesex
" John, moulder, house Alfred do.
Hamor Benjamin, farmer, house Salem, K. D.
Hanaford Charles O. house Chestnut
Handy Willard A. moulder, house off 62 Water
HANNAFORD FREDERICK P. (McDonald & Hannaford, harness makers,) house Milk c. Chestnut, C. D.
Hanscom Aaron B. machinist, house 20 Pleasant
Hardy John, machinist, boards Thomas P. Wills
Hargraves Richard, emp. Davis & Furber, boards Samuel Diggle
Harlow Samuel A. house Osgood
Harper Catherine Mrs. house Sutton near Main
" Lawrence, farm hand, house Osgood, R. D.
Harriman Rose Mrs. house G. H. Tuttle
Harrington Isabella Mrs. (John) house Mrs. Robertina Crockett
" Patrick, laborer, house Sargent
Harris George L. books, stationery, etc. Water, house Church near Water
" Henry Mrs. house Samuel Goff
Hartley John, foreman finishing room No. Andover mill, house Main opp. Second
" John G. overseer of dressing, house Mrs. Mary A. do.
" Mary A. Mrs. (George) house off Osgood near Pleasant
" Samuel, emp. Sutton mill, house Water, 10 Yellow Row
Hartmann Nicholas, spinner, house Ellis block, Main
Hartwell Fred, mechanic, house off Andover, C. D.
Harvey Hiram, laborer, house Salem, K. D.
Hathorn George E. emp. card clothing dept. at Davis & Furber's, house Third c. Middle
" Mary E. house George E. do.
Haverty John J. cloth finisher, house Mrs. Mary do.
" Mary Mrs. (John) house Second
" Michael J. emp. Washington mill, house Mrs. Mary do.
" Thomas E. house Mrs. Mary do.
" William P. machinist, house Mrs. Mary do.
Hayes John, weaver, boards John Wilton
" Sarah M. Mrs. (Dudley) house W. H. Hayes
" Walter, machinist, house 20 East Water
" Walter H. farmer, house Osgood, R. D.

Physicians' Prescriptions are guaranteed to be compounded from THE BEST QUALITY OF MEDICINE,

Hayward William B. house Osgood
Healy Patrick, laborer, house Main near Osgood
Henry Susan, house Mrs. Ellen T. Morrissey
Herbert John, machinist, house Patrick do.
" Maurice, paymaster Stevens mill, house Patrick do.
" Patrick, emp. Stevens mill, house Stevens near Pleasant
Herod Mrs. Alice (William) house 32 East Water
Hesters Frank, emp. Stevens mill, boards Isaac Nason
Heywood James, woolen dresser, house Stevens near Pleasant
Heyworeth John, house 5 Beverly
Hill Richard O. machinist, house Brown's court
Hinchcliffe Joseph A. second hand weaving room Sutton mill, house Sutton
Hinman Edward P. signal tender B. & M. R. R. h. Marblehead
Hinxman Superbus D. blacksmith, house Belmont corner Hodges
Hirst Brook. loom fixer, house Lawrence
Hoban Austin J. foreman spinning room, house Phillips court near Pleasant
Holiday William, machinist, house 14 Water
Holmes Charles M. machinist, house 28 East Water
" John W. emp. Davis & Furber, house Charles M. do.
Holt Albert N. summer boarding house, house Prospect. C. D.
" Augusta M. emp. Davis & Furber, house William C. do.
" Edna M. stenographer, house William C. do.
" Peter, farmer, house Salem near Marble Ridge station
" Peter, Jr. house Salem near Marble Ridge station
" Sophronia E. house James A. Montgomery
Holt William C. carpenter, house opp. 6 Pleasant
Hopkins George E. farmer, house Church
Howarth James, watchman Davis & Furber, house 69 Water
Howe Albert, card setter, house High
Howes Claydon, coachman, house M. T. Stevens place
Hughes Stephen, foreman of yard, Davis & Furber, h. 1 Water
" Winfield S. farmer and milk dealer, house Essex, P. D.
Hulme Charles W. house Water
Hume George, house 7 Beverly
Humphrey James R. night watchman E. C. S. h. Second cor. Main
Hurst Brook, house Lawrence
Hutchinson Oliver S. station agent Ingalls Crossing, house Stephen W. Ingalls
Hyde Isaac, house Rev. Charles Noyes

ABSOLUTELY PURE, and IN STRICT ACCORDANCE with Physicians' orders, at **Perkins'.**

I

ILLSLEY ISAAC, clerk, house Stevens near Salem, C. D.
Ingalls Daniel F. farmer, house Henry P. do.
"   Henry P. house Johnson
"   John E. carpenter, house Stevens near Salem
"   Stephen W. farmer, house Salem, Ingalls Crossing
"   Williams, carpenter, boards Mrs. Kate Kilburn
Ivory John, machinist, boards Ezra A. Carter

J

JACKSON CALVIN V. junk dealer, house 23 Beverly
"   David H. carder, house Greene c. Poor's lane
"   Vernon H. boards 23 Beverly
JACOBS J. coal and lumber, office and yard Main n. Sutton, residence Peabody
Jagger Fred, house Winter
"   Henry, house Salem
"   Theophilus, house Stevens
Jenkins Alfred F. house Dale
"   B. F. farmer, house Dale, P. D.
"   H. Fred, machinist, house Maple av.
"   Milton S. farmer, house Dale, P. D.
"   Samuel A. machinist, house High near Sutton
"   Samuel C. carpenter, house 11 East Water
Jenness George A. painter, house School
Jennings Annie, house George W. Dunnils
Jensen Christian, pattern maker, house 21 Pleasant
Jewett Charles E. machinist, house Hezekiah do.
"   Hezekiah, machinist, house Marblehead
Johnson Catherine, house Stevens near Osgood
"   Charles F. farmer, house Stevens near Salem
"   Gardner, farmer, house Turnpike, F. D.
"   James T. house Depot, C. D.
"   Thomas, machinist, house Clarendon corner Water
"   William A. carpenter, house High
"   William R. machinist, house Church near Water
Jones Lawrence B. ice man, house Frank M. Greenwood
Josselyn George C. proprietor Josselyn's Express, house 25 Pleasant
"   Isaiah B. house Marblehead
Joyce Patrick, house Ashland near railroad station
"   Redmon A. machinist, boards Patrick do.
"   William P. house Main

Perfumery, Toilet and Medicinal Soaps,

K

KAY GEORGE, cotton spinner, house Marblehead c. Middlesex
Keating John, machinist, house Water near engine house
" Mary Mrs. (Patrick) house Water near engine house
Keefe Arthur, house Maple av.
" James O. blacksmith, house Ashland n. railroad station
" John A. machinist, house Maple av.
" Thomas, house Ashland
" Thomas J. house Maple av.
Keegan Patrick, house Second
Keenan William, machinist, house Ellis block, Main
Kelley Charles J. blacksmith, house Third near Main
" Edward J. hairdresser Water, house do.
" Eliza Mrs. (Jeffrey) house Main opp. Public Library
" Joseph, fireman Davis & Furber, bds. Mrs. Kate Kilburn
" Mary E. weaver, house Mrs. Eliza do.
" Nellie T. weaver, house Mrs. Eliza do.
" Patrick, laborer, house Middlesex corner Third
" William F. printer, house Mrs. Eliza do.
Kelsey Harry, emp. Davis & Furber, house Dr. Frank E. Weil
Kemp Ernest, emp. Davis & Furber, house 45 East Water
Keniston George A. machinist, house Main opp. Catholic church
" Henry, mason, house Main near Merrimac
" Lydia A. Mrs. (Orrin) house Main opp. Catholic church
Kennedy John, emp. Davis & Furber, house 33 East Water
Kennelley James, machinist, boards Maggie do.
" John C. machinist, boards Maggie do.
" Maggie, house Ashland near railroad station
" William E. machinist, boards Maggie do.
Kenney George, groom, house Lake View farm
Kershaw Abraham, wool sorter, house Stevens
" John G. wool scourer, house Sutton near railroad station
" John P. moulder, house Ashland opp. railroad station
" Robert, section hand, house Middlesex
Kilburn Kate Mrs. (Benjamin) house Main opp. school house
Kiley John, house 51 East Water
Killay Patrick, laborer, house Thomas do.
" Thomas, machinist, house Perry
Kimball Charlotte G. house Andover, C. D.
" Henry T. clerk Shreve, Crump & Low, h. Andover, C. D.
" John, grocer, house Marblehead
" Maria D. teacher, house Miss Charlotte D. do.
" Rosina Mrs. (Seth) house Oliver R. Gile
Kinnear Theodore H. painter, house Salem Turnpike

Sponges, Chamois Skins. Perkins, the Druggist.

Kirk John F. painter, house Sutton near railroad station
Kittredge Hannah A. house Prospect, C. D.
" Henrietta F. Mrs. (Joseph) house Prospect, C. D.
" Romeo, machinist, house Marblehead
" Sarah, house Prospect, C. D.
" Simeon J. emp. Davis & Furber, house Water
Knapp George F. laborer, house Depot, C. D.
Krieling Frank J. carpenter, house 14 Beverly

L

LACY LAWRENCE G. house Cedar
Lamb James, house 40 East Water
Lambert Bozin, house Sutton
" Henry, farm hand, house off Pleasant, Stevens Village
" Henry, laborer, house Boxford, K. D.
Lamere Frederick H. bookkeeper, house Joseph H. do.
" Mary H. dressmaker, house Joseph H. do.
" Joseph H. iron moulder, house Clarendon opp. Water
" Lawrence, house Water
" L. William, iron moulder, h. Marblehead c. Middlesex
Lancaster John, finisher, boards Tom do.
" Tom, tinsmith, house 31 East Water
Lane Mary, domestic, house James J. Finnegan
" Patrick, emp. Charles Wilcox, boards do.
Lanigan Edward J. house Union
" Lawrence, spinner, house Greene c. Middlesex
Lawler James E. iron moulder, house Main near junc. Water
" Michael, emp. Stevens & Sons, house White Row
Lawless Thomas J. machinist, house Railroad near Union
Laycock John, machinist, house Maple av.
Leach James, weaver, house Water, 15 Yellow Row
Leary Arthur, laborer, house Ashland c. Ferry
Leaver Thomas, house foot Maple av.
Lee Philip, blacksmith, boards Charles Wilcox
" Tom, machinist, house 3 Water
Leighton George L. carpenter, house 36 East Water
" Joseph L. painter, house Second c. Main
LEITCH JAMES W. stoves, ranges, plumbing, etc. Water, house Maple av.
Leonard Frank S. machinist, house Water
Lewis Fred, emp. Davis & Furber, boards 58 Water
" John B. house Pleasant
Leycock George, house 57 East Water
Ligget Samuel, machinist, house Main junc. Water

Fine Confectionery, Stationery, Pocket Knives and Razors. PERKINS, the DRUGGIST.

Lindsay John, dresser, house Maple av. c. Second
Littlefield Daniel, house Main
Lobbel Bozin, moulder, house Sutton near Main
Long Elizabeth Mrs. (Elijah) house Marble Ridge District
" Henry A. farmer, house Boxford, K. D.
Longworth James, emp. Davis & Furber, house 44 East Water
Lord John, house Stevens
" Margaret J. Mrs. (William) house Second n. Railroad
Loring George B. house Prospect
" John A. house Prospect
" John O. house Prospect
Lovejoy Albert, engineer Davis & Furber, house off 6 Water
Lowe John, painter and paper hanger, house Main opp. Second
Lynch Mary Mrs. (Timothy) house Main near First
" Patrick, iron moulder, house Second near Main
Lyons Frank, house Pond
" Oscar, house Pond

M

MACKIE DAVID, house Second corner Maple av.
" Joseph, emp. Stevens mill, house White Row
" William, overseer weaving room, Sutton mill, house Sutton near Sutton mill
Magoon Martin, machinist, boards Mrs. W. B. Perkins
Mahoney Cornelius, emp. Davis & Furber, house 52 East Water
MAHONEY ELLEN MRS. groceries and dry goods, 35 East Water, house do.
" Jeremiah J. house Water
" John P. S. house Water
" M. J. in summer house Chestnut
Manchester Frederick, loom fixer, house William do.
" Matthew H. student, house William do.
" William, loom fixer, house Middlesex near Lawrence
Manion Brion Mrs. house Maple av.
" James, coachman, house John do.
" John, house Osgood
" Margaret C. emp. G. W. Berrian, boards do.
Manning Nedson D. machinist, house First
" Harriet Mrs. (Eldredge G.) house Elm near Pleasant
" Harriet E. teacher piano-forte, house Mrs. Harriet do.
" John, section hand B. & M. R. R. bds. Daniel H. Ready
" John, 2d, farmer, house Johnson, C. D.
Mansfield Marshall, house Cedar
Marden Patrick, house Dale

Our assortment of TOOTH BRUSHES cannot be beat. **Perkins, the Druggist.**

Markey Alba M. emp. Davis & Furber, house Second n. Main
Marshall Richard C. emp. B. & M. R. R. house 15 Beverly
Marston Della, teacher piano-forte, house John B. do.
"   George A. overseer Davis & Furber, house Prescott
"   John B. overseer Davis & Furber, house Prescott
Marvin Frederick, finisher, house Stevens, Stevens Village
Maslen Abraham J. house 17 Beverly
"   David, house Beverly
"   John, machinist, house Main, opp. M. E. church
Massey John, house Dale
Mattheson George, farm hand, house Stevens near Osgood
Matthews Henry Rev. pastor Methodist Episcopal church, house Main corner Merrimac
Mayer Samuel R. motorman, house Main opp. First
McAloon Margaret Mrs. house Second near Main
"   Owen, house Second
"   William F. machinist, house Mrs. Margaret do.
McCabe Sarah Mrs. (Francis) house Main near First
McCartan Hugh, machinist, house 18 East Water
McCarthy Charles, emp. Davis & Furber, house Railroad near Maple av.
"   Hannah Mrs. (John) house Water opp. engine house
"   Henry B. machinist, house Second near Main
"   Timothy A. machinist, house Second corner Main
McCarty Jerry F. machinist, house Mrs. Katherine do.
"   Katherine Mrs. (Dennis) house Marblehead
"   Patrick, flagman B. & M. R. R. house foot River View
McClary Thomas J. overseer Davis & Furber, house 18 Elm opp. Pleasant
McDermott Patrick, farm hand, house George Matthesou
McDONALD ALBERT, (McDonald & Hannaford, harness makers,) Andover, house Andover, C. D.
"   Ann Mrs. (Bartholomew) house First
"   Dennis, house Railroad c. Sargent
"   Edward P. emp. North Andover mill, h. Second c. Main
"   Eugene C. laborer, house Mrs. Mary do.
"   Hannah, house Mrs. Mary do.
"   Harriet Mrs. (James P.) house Andover, C. D.
"   Jeremiah, moulder, house Michael do.
"   Maggie, bookkeeper, house Mrs. Mary do.
"   Mary Mrs. (Cornelius) house opp. 1 Water
"   Michael, teamster, house Sutton near Sutton mill
"   William, machinist, house Michael do.
McDonough Patrick, laborer, house 24 River View
"   Mary Mrs. (Daniel) house Patrick H. Curley

Upon the Purity of Drugs and the reliability of our work we depend. **PERKINS, THE DRUGGIST.**

McDuffie Daniel, farmer, house Railroad corner Greene
" John, moulder, house Daniel do.
McEchrearn Catherine B. domestic, house Samuel D. Stevens
McElwaise George, house 8 Beverly
McEvoy James, emp. Davis & Furber, h. Second n. Railroad st.
" Patrick, clerk, house Salem corner Stevens, C. D.
" Richard M. emp. Davis & Furber, house Second near Railroad
McGovern Thomas, house Stevens
McGrail Peter, machinist, house 50 East Water
McGregor Alexander, laborer, boards Mrs. Kate Kilburn
McInnis Lewis, house Main
McKenna Alexander, house Stevens
McKinnon Alexander, laborer, house White Row
" Donald, emp. M. T. Stevens, house Stevens
McKone Ellen Mrs. (Edward) house Water near Elm
" Francis E. (F. McKone & Co.) coal dealer, house Water near Elm
McLean Andrew, machinist, house 15 Pleasant
" Elizabeth, house Swinton do.
" Swinton, house 15 Pleasant
McNiff Thomas, house Middlesex
" William, machinist, boards Thomas do.
McNulty John B. spinner, house Water, 1 Yellow Row
McPherson Charles, emp. Davis & Furber, boards 9 Water
" Timothy, teamster Davis & Furber, house 9 Water
McQueston Solon F. machinist, house Church
" William M. electrician, house Solon F. do.
McRobbie John, machinist, boards George Wilton
Mead Harlow Mrs. house Foster, P. D.
Meehan John, emp. Stevens mill, boards John Wilton
Mehan John, coachman Eben Sutton, boards Ezra A. Carter
" Patrick, laborer, boards Ezra A. Carter
Mendonca Manuel, house Lawrence near Middlesex
Merrifield George, farm hand, house William Gemmell
Merrill Charles F. emp. Pemberton mill, house Main c. Sutton
" Moses, emp. card clothing room, Davis & Furber, house 23 Pleasant
Merrow Charles F. house Sutton c. Main
Meserve Charles E. meat and provisions, Pleasant, house Main near First
" David H. farmer, house Andover, near Andover line
" Delphena, bookkeeper, house John N. do.
" John N. teaming and jobbing, house Pleasant n. Davis
" Mosher B. house Andover

For Quality and Price PERKINS' Extract Jamaica Ginger leads them all. **PERKINS, THE DRUGGIST.**

Midwood Joseph, sexton St. Paul Episcopal church, house Main
Miller James B. emp. Pemberton mill, house Lawrence near Middlesex
" John B. painter, house 19 Beverly
Mills Emma A. Mrs. (John H.) house Pleasant near Davis
" John, house White Row
" John, machinist, boards Mrs. Ann Blanchard
" Walsingham R. moulder, house Frank R. Prince
Milner Maude, supervisor of drawing, house Thomas do.
" Rebecca Mrs. house 66 Water corner Church
" Thomas, supt. card clothing dept. Davis & Furber, house Stonington
" William S. machinist, house Mrs. Rebecca do.
Milnes John T. house Pleasant
Mitchel David, machinist, house Main opp. First
Mizen Annie V. house Mrs. Sarah do.
" George H. hostler, house Water near engine house
" Sarah Mrs. (John H.) house Cross
Monaghan Kate, domestic, house Hon. William A. Russell
Montgomery James A. farmer, house Osgood, R. D.
Moody Edwin W. bookkeeper M. T. Stevens & Sons, house Salem, C. D.
" Wedgewood, gardener, house Lake View farm
Moore George W. machinist, boards William C. do.
" William C. machinist, house 21 Beverly
Morgan George W. moulder, house Elm near Main
" James, laborer, house Ashland opp. railroad
" John A. house Ashland
Morrill Charles H. student, house Dr. Charles P. do.

M ORRILL CHARLES P., M. D. physician and surgeon, office and residence Elm c. Cross, office hours before 9 a. m., 1 to 2 and 7 to 8 p. m.

Morris John, watchman, house Second c. Railroad
Morrison James, engineer, boards Joseph Greenwood
Morrisey Thomas F. coachman, house Gen. Sutton place

If you want Patent Medicines at cut-rate prices, (guaranteed genuine,) go to PERKINS, the Druggist.

MORRISSEY ELLEN T. MRS. restaurant and boarding, house Main opp. First
" John A. insurance agent, house 13 Water
" Susie T. clerk, house Mrs. Ellen T. do.
" Thomas, dresser, boards Mrs. Kate Kilburn
" Thomas, coachman, house Andover, C. D.
Morse Clarissa, house Johnson, C. D.
Morss Jacob W. house Third near Main
" Walter S. emp. Gilman Bros. Bradford, h. Third n. Main
Morton Charles, house Main corner Sargent court
" Alice H. Mrs. (William) house First
" Ann Mrs. (George) house Water near Church
" James, machinist, house Water, 14 Yellow Row
" John, laborer, house Water near Church
Moulton George H. machinist, boards Calvin M. Sanborn
" D. A. emp. Maverick Oil Co. house High c. Prescott
Mowat John, emp. Davis & Furber, house 53 East Water
Murch Lewis, house Second c. Maple av.
" William F. foreman at Davis & Furber's, h. 8 Pleasant
Murphy Dennis J. spinner, house foot Sargent
" James, coachman, house Lake View farm
" James F. moulder, house Main opp. First
" James W. iron moulder, boards Charles McCarthy
" John, engineer North Andover mill, house Main near railroad crossing
" John, moulder, house Patrick do.
" John L. foreman Sutton's farm, house Main c. Railroad
" Katie, milliner, house Patrick do.
" Lawrence, emp. Stevens mill, h. Water, 5 Yellow Row
" Michael, coachman, house 2 Water
" Patrick, farm hand, house John L. do.
" Patrick, emp. Davis & Furber, house Second
" Patrick F. variety store Main n. railroad crossing, h. do.
" Stephen, house Patrick F. do.
" Timothy, coachman, house Stevens, C. D.
" William, machinist, house Michael do.
Murray Amelia, domestic, house James A. Montgomery

N

NASON RUBY S. MRS. (James) house John Barker
" Mary E. teacher, house John Barker
" Isaac, emp. Stevens mill, house White Row
Nelson John, machinist, house opp. 3 Pleasant

If you have a tired feeling after seeing **Perkins, the Druggist,** on all these pages, buy a bottle of his superior Beef, Wine and Iron.

Nesbit Rocena (John) house Joseph W. Fountain
Newhall Charles A. coal dealer in Lynn, house Johnson
Newton John, polisher, house School
Nichols Harrison, farmer, house Foster, P. D.
" Silas, laborer, house Foster, P. D.
" William H. house Foster
Norman Joseph, carpenter, house 33 East Water
Noyes Charles Rev. pastor of the Unitarian church, house Chestnut, C. D.
" George R. student, house Rev. Charles do.
Nutting Ellen M. Mrs. (D. Wallace) house Chestnut, C. D.
" Esther M. house Mrs. Ellen M. do.

O

OATES EZRA, farmer, house Salem, K. D.
O'Brien Ann Mrs. (Jeremiah) house John A. Sullivan
" Bartholomew, coachman S. M. Stevens, h. White Row
" James, machinist, house Mrs. John do.
" John, laborer, house Ashland opp. railroad station
" John Jr. house Ashland
" John, house Mrs. John do.
" Mrs. John, house Osgood
" Timothy, laborer, house Perry
O'Connors Daniel, laborer, house Ashland
Oddy Paikinison, house White Row
O'Donald Margaret Mrs. (Murphy) house Ellis block, Main
" Michael, moulder, house Ellis block, Main
Ogden Joseph, tinsmith, house Sutton near Sagehomme & Byers' mill
O'Leary Arthur, house Ashland
Oliver Margaret Mrs. (James O.) house Sutton n. railroad station
Osgood Aaron B. machinist, house Elm near Main
" Annie M. teacher, house Aaron B. do.
" Horace C. photographer, house Aaron B. do.
" Isaac P. postmaster, house Osgood
" L. Edgar, local editor Andover Townsman, Depot postoffice, house Elm
Otter Samuel, emp. Stevens mill, boards John Wilton
Oxton Frank E. conductor electric railroad, house Ashland opp. railroad station

P

PAGE WILLIAM D. teamster, house Church near Water
Paine George N. carpenter, house Merrimac near Water

❋ PERKINS, ❋ THE ❋ DRUGGIST. ❋

Parker Arthur, house Stevens Village
Patchett Joseph, house Sutton
Paterson James, house 14 Pleasant
Paul Charles W. house Cedar
" James, emp. H. M. Whitney, house near H. M. Whitney
" William H. emp. Sutton mill, boards Robert Wilcox
Peabody Bertha, domestic, house Charles A. Newhall
Peak Charles A. emp. A. P. Fuller, boards do.
Pearson George, machinist, boards Thomas P. Wills
Pelham John, house Pelham
Pendlebury Thomas, carpenter, house School

PERKINS GEORGE H. druggist, Main, house Main opp. engine house
" Mary E. Mrs. (Apollos L.) house Church
" W. B. Mrs. co-operative boarding house, h. 1 Pleasant
Perley Edwin L. clerk North Andover mill, house Main opp. public library
" Leverett S. overseer spindle room, Davis & Furber, house Main opp. public library
Perry John, painter, house Perry c. Pelham
Phelan John, machinist, house 42 East Water
" Martin, emp. Sutton's mill, house First
" Maurice, house 49 East Water
Phelps Charles W. blacksmith, house Marblehead
" Eliza Mrs. (Henry) house Church
" Henry W. house Salem
" William W. emp. G. W. Berrian, boards do.
Philbrick John, machinist, boards Mrs. W. B. Perkins
Phillips John, carpenter, house 9 Pleasant
Phipps Laura M. Mrs. (Joseph) house Andover, C. D.
Piessey Joseph, farmer, house Lawrence near Middlesex
Pike John R. machinist, rooms Catherine Bradley
Pilling Charles A. postmaster, house Sutton near railroad station
Pinkham Hollis C. boards Mrs. Eliza S. Sargent
Pollard John, house Pleasant
Poor Charles H. emp. Mrs. Sarah E. Way, boards do.
" James C. farmer, house Sutton near Whitney
Porter William S. machinist, house 63 Water
Powell Eldred, laborer, house Suffolk corner Beverly
Prescott Abbott, carpenter, house High
" Lucy Mrs. (James) house High corner Prescott
" Mary, house Mrs. Lucy do.
Pressey Joseph, house Lawrence
Preston Benjamin J. house Osgood
" Christina Mrs. (Jonas) house John D. Preston

Hair, Tooth, Nail and Shaving Brushes at all prices.   PERKINS, the Druggist.

Preston John D. machinist, house High near Sutton
Pride William, machinist, boards Mrs. W. B. Perkins
Prince Frank L. supt. Davis & Furber foundry, house High
Pulsifer Martin H. machinist, house Maple av.
Putnam Joseph H. iron moulder, house Maple av.

Q

QUAMBY BETSEY MRS. (Joseph) house Thomas Radcliffe
Quealy Catherine T. emp. Davis & Furber, house Mrs. Ellen do.
" Ellen Mrs. (Edward) house Elm corner Pleasant
" Hannah, librarian, house Mrs. Ellen do.
" John C. machinist, house Maple av.
" John T. dyer, house Main corner Sutton
" Mary Mrs. (Michael) house Maple av.
" Mary E. teacher, house Mrs. Ellen do.
Quinton William F. moulder, house Pleasant

R

RABS FREDERICK, house Forest
Radcliffe John, weaver, house Sutton near Main
" Thomas, machinist, house Main near railroad crossing
Rand Jennie A. Mrs. (Joseph A.) house Water, 16 Yellow Row
Raycroft James A. emp. W. A. Russell, house Lake View farm
Rea Calvin, farmer, house Foster, P. D.
" F. Orris, farmer, house off Johnson, F. D.
" Frank H. house Bradford
" George, farmer, house Turnpike, F. D.
" Hannah B. Mrs. (Aaron G.) house Second c. Maple av.
" John H. carpenter and builder, house Osgood junc. Main
" John H. Mrs. preserved fruits and jellies, Osgood junc. Main, house do.
" Letitia A. boards Mrs. Hannah B. do.
" Olive A. house John H. do.
" Sarah Letitia, house Orris do.
" Susan Mrs. (Jacob C.) house Orris do.
" William H. carpenter, house Belmont
Ready Daniel H. section foreman, house Ingalls Crossing
Reagan Daniel J. house Michael do.
" Joseph J. operative Stevens mill, house First
" Michael, farmer, house Merrimac near Water
Reardon Patrick, laborer, house Osgood
Reeves Andrew, house Pleasant near Davis
" Peter, sausage manufacturer, Lawrence, house Pleasant

PERKINS, the Druggist, has recommendations from the leading physicians.

Regan James, house Union near Railroad
Reid Harold C. emp. Sutton's mill, house Ronald M. do.
" Ronald M. laborer, house 23 Main
Reilly Henry, teamster, house Belmont
" Henry P. carpenter, boards Henry do.
" Samuel M. machinist, boards Henry do.
REXTROW GEORGE, painter and paper-hanger, Church, house do.
Reynolds Clarence W. house Maple av.
REYNOLDS EDWIN O. cider manufacturer, house Judson E. do.
" George, emp. Davis & Furber, house 47 East Water
REYNOLDS JUDSON E. cider manufacturer, house Johnson, F. D.
" W. C. house Stonington
Rhodes Elizabeth Mrs. (Joseph) house Sutton opp. Sagehomme & Byers' mill
Rice Robert, woolen dresser, house Mrs. Donnelly
RICHARDSON JOHN W. groceries, flour, etc., Main c. Third, house do.
RICHARDSON JOHN W., JR. clerk J. W. Richardson, house do.
" Patrick, emp. Stevens mill, boards John Wilton
Riel Joseph, machinist, house 5 Water
Roach Helen E. teacher, house James A. do.
" James, emp. Stevens mill, house David Bell
" James A. carpenter, house 26 Pleasant
" John F. principal Southboro school, house James A. do.
Roberts William, tinsmith, house 64 Water
Robertson Arthur G. house Sutton
Robinson Addison M. house Stevens near Osgood
" Charles H. bookkeeper Sutton's mill, house Main near railroad crossing
" Enos S. machinist, house Sutton near Sutton's mill
" Joseph, confectioner, Lawrence, house Middlesex
" Julia M. emp. Sutton's mill, house Enos S. do.
" Richard, house Railroad
" Nathan, dresser, house Sutton near Sutton mill
" William, emp. Davis & Furber, house 10 Water
" William B. commercial salesman, house Andover, C. D.
" William H. machinist, house Sutton opp. Sagehomme & Byers mill
Rock Alfred, house River
Roebuck George, machine polisher, house Second near Main
Rogers George A. supt. Cochichewick farm, h. J. D. W. French

Strictly pure articles, and exactly as represented, is the reputation of **PERKINS, THE DRUGGIST.**

Rokes Menander L. emp. Davis & Furber, house Railroad near Second
Roundy William S. shoemaker, house Osgood, C. D.
Royal Fred, harness maker, house Osgood
" George F. house Osgood
Royds James, house Maple av.
Ruggles Willard, emp. W. J. Cheever, boards do.
Rundlett John D. house Maple av.
" William D. draughtsman, house 7 Maple av.
Russell Hon. William A. house Lake View farm
Ryan John, laborer, house Main near Osgood
" Mary, house Miss Catherine Johnson
" Patrick, machinist, house John do.
" Patrick J. core maker, house Main c. Davis
" Robert, moulder, house 37 East Water
" Thomas J. machinist, house John do.

S

SANBORN ANNIE E. teacher, house Joseph S. do.
" Calvin M. machinist, house Maple av. c. Second
SANBORN JOHN F. baker, house Stonington
" Joseph S. overseer mule room, Davis & Furber, house Third c. Maple av.
" Mary J. Mrs. (William) house Calvin M. do.
Sanderson James, farm hand, house Lake View farm
Sanford Howard, house Osgood
" Maurice, house Bradford
Sargent Annie L. teacher, house Mrs. Caroline A. do.
" Caroline A. Mrs. (Isaac C.) house Pleasant c. Clarendon
" Edmund D. moulder, house High near Sutton
" Eliza S. Mrs. house Belmont
SARGENT FRED L. boarding stable, boards Mrs. Eliza S. do.
" Helen C. teacher, house Mrs. Caroline A. do.
Saunders Annie W. clerk Brooks Bros. Haverhill, house James do.
" Benjamin P. foreman forge room Davis & Furber, house Elm near Cross
" Charles, painter, boards Charles Dame
" Elizabeth M. teacher of piano-forte and soprano soloist, house Benjamin P. do.
" Frank H. collector, house Benjamin P. do.
" George W. drug clerk, house James do.
" James, machinist, house 18 Pleasant

LIQUIDONIA, FOR CHAPPED HANDS, is of more value for the money

Sawyer Thomas P. carpenter, house 25 Elm
Schofield James Mrs. variety store, Main, house do.
" James, emp. Sutton's mill, house Main near Second
" James, house Railroad
" John, cloth finisher, house 31 River View
Scraghan Hugh, emp. Stevens mill, boards John Wilton
Schrunder Henry, laborer, house off Osgood near Pleasant
Scott David, painter, boards Charles Dame
Severance Martha Mrs. (Joshua) house Edmund D. Sargent
Shanahan Michael F. watchman No. Andover mill, house Water, 12 Yellow Row
Sharpe John W. hairdresser, Water, house 39 East Water
Sharpner George L. house Forest
" George M. house Forest
Shaw George H. iron moulder, house 22 East Water
Sheahan Michael, watchman, boards John J. Donnelly
" William, dresser, house Sutton near railroad station
Shearer Hugh, machinist, house Lawrence corner Middlesex
" John M. machinist, house Hugh do.
Sheed Charles J. H. machinist, house Church
Sheehan Michael, house River
Shepard Joseph, house Third corner Maple av.
Sherlock Thomas, laborer, house 29 River View
Shuttleworth William, house Middlesex corner Lawrence
Silloway George W. clerk J. W. Richardson, residence Methuen
Simpson Lydia A. Mrs. (Samuel W.) house Maple av.
Sleigh Isaac, blacksmith, house Perry c. Pelham
Small Ella A. teacher, boards Miss Charlotte G. Kimball
Smith Alfred L. principal Merrimack school, boards Mrs. Harriet Manning
" Alonzo, farmer, house Boston road, F. D.
" Ann Mrs. (George) house Main opp. Railroad
" Bradford C. road commissioner, house rear Charles B. Smith's, Elm
" Charles B. machinist, house Elm near Main
" Edward H. house Prospect, C. D.
" Elizabeth Mrs. (Jonas) house Morton
" Ernest L. house Elm
" Francis Capt. emp. Davis & Furber, boards Charles J. Kelley
" Fred S. student, house George I. do.
" George A. blacksmith, house High
" George I. machinist, house Third corner Main
" Henry R. laborer, house Sutton near Post-Office
" H. H. D. machinist, boards Mrs. W. B. Perkins

Than any other article of its kind. 25 cents a bottle, at **PERKINS', the Druggist.**

Smith James, house River View
" James, machinist, house Mrs. Ann do.
" James H. farm hand, boards Ezra A. Carter
" John F. house Second
" John J. machinist, house Main opp. Railroad
" John H. D. treasurer Boston Belting Co. h. Prospect, C. D.
" Peter, carpenter, house Mrs. Ann do.
" Richard H. house Main
" Richard R. emp. Standard Oil Co. house Marblehead near railroad
" Robert B. house H. M. Whitney
" Samuel, house Stevens, C. D.
" William D. watchman Davis & Furber, h. 41 East Water
" William H. iceman, house Stevens
" William M. house Timothy A. McCarthy
Somerville John, blacksmith, house Pleasant
" John, Jr. house John do.
Soraghan Hugh, house Water
Spence George S. house Main c. School
Spofford Charlotte, house Miss Catherine Johnson
" Eliza, house Miss Catherine Johnson
" William H. emp. B. & M. R. R. house Marblehead
Sproul Mary B. teacher, boards A. N. Holt, C. D.
Stansfield Charles E. clerk, house Elm near Main
Stark Lynde A. foreman Lake View farm, house do.
" Samuel W. house Bradford
Sarrett Levi R. farmer, house Johnson, F. D.
Standring James, sexton Methodist church, house Elm n. Main
STEARNS CHARLES S. druggist Main, house do.

Stevens Anna M. Mrs. (Horace N.) house Prospect
" Byron, house Water
" Fannie H. house Mrs. Anna M. do.
" George, tinsmith, house Main opp. Merrimac
" Horace N. with Faulkner, Page & Co. house Prospect
" John, house Main near Third
" John F. house Main near Third
" Kate H. house Mrs. Anna M. do.
" Moses T. (M. T. Stevens & Sons) woolen manufacturer, house Stevens
" Moses T. Jr. (with M. T. Stevens & Sons) house Moses T. do.
" Nathaniel (M. T. Stevens & Sons) house Stevens
" Oliver, house Marble Ridge Farm, Essex
" Samuel D. (M. T. Stevens & Sons) house Stevens

DR. BIGELOW'S GREAT ENGLISH COUGH CURE is the

Stevens Susan P. house Mrs. Anna M. do.
Stewart Andrew, house Bradford
" Hugh, machinist, house 19 Pleasant
" Mary Mrs. (Hugh) house 19 Pleasant
" William J. machinist, house 19 Pleasant
Stickney Melvin D. farm hand, house Osgood, R. D.
Stiles Daniel P. farmer, house Andover road, F. D.
" Horace A. carpenter, house 27 Beverly
" Warren, farmer, house Andover road, F. D.
" William A. farmer, house Andover road, F. D.
Stillings Charles E. bookkeeper Davis & Furber, house Third
Stone George, machinist, house Osgood near Pleasant
" John, house Sutton
" Joseph H. (Davis & Furber) house Greene
" Joseph H. Mrs. house Joseph H. do.
" Walter G. machinist, house 3 Pleasant
Stoodley Annie M. bookkeeper T. A. Holt & Co. house Andover
" Ruby F. Mrs. (Henry) house Andover, C. D.
Starmont William, boiler maker, house Pleasant corner Clarendon
Stott Abraham, watchman, house 21 East Water
" Arthur W. bookkeeper, house Abraham do.
" Isaac, spinner, house Church near Water
Stritch Richard, house Perry
Stromblad John A. machinist, h. over A. P. Currier's store, Water
Sullivan Catherine Mrs. (Bartholomew) house School
" Edward W. house Railroad
" Eugene T. painter, house Mrs. Catherine do.
" John A. iron moulder, house foot Belmont
" John W. machinist, house Mrs. Catherine do.
" Mary Mrs. house John F. Stevens
" Patrick, baggage master B. & M. station, boards John C. Carter
" Richard, house Court
" Timothy, laborer, house Railroad
Sutcliffe Daniel W. boss dyer, house Main
" Joseph, machinist, house Main near railroad crossing
Sutton Mary H. Mrs. (Gen. Eben) house Johnson
" William, house Johnson
Swanson Swan, house Essex
Sweeney John, machinist, house Pelham
" John, house 24 Marblehead
" John J. machinist, house Perry
" P. J. plumber, Lawrence, house 24 Marblehead
Symonds Frederick, house Symonds

Best Remedy on the market. 25 Cents, at **PERKINS', the Druggist.**

T

TARBOX CLARISSA MRS. (Ephraim) house Daniel W. Carney
Tattersall Albert, painter, house Middlesex
" Joseph H. painter and paper-hanger, house Samuel do.
" Samuel, machinist, house Second near Main
Taylor Joseph R. machinist, house School
Tempest Joseph, emp. Pacific mill, Lawrence, house Davis
Thomas Albert, machinist, boards Mrs. Ellen T. Morrissey
" Eliza Mrs. (Richard) house Ferry
Thompson Aaron D. farmer and station agent, house Dale, C. D.
" Charles D. wool sorter, house Marblehead, near railroad
" James, machinist, house James G. do.
" James G. watchman Davis & Furber, house off 61 Water
" James M. machinist, house 11 Pleasant
" John, house James G. do.
" John, machinist, boards Thomas P. Wills
" Thomas, house Pleasant
" Walter, machinist, boards Thomas P. Wills
Thornton James, spinner, boards Joseph W. Emmett
Tibbetts Herbert B. house Marblehead
Tisdale Frank F. card setter, house 16 Pleasant
Tobin Cornelius, emp. Davis & Furber, bds. Mrs. Ellen Mahoney
Toohey William J. house Stevens
Toole James L. house Second
" Thomas H. house Sutton
Toomey Michael, house First
Toothacher A. G. house Maple av.
Towle James, wool sorter, boards Patrick P. Daw
Towne George W. house Johnson, C. D.
" Horace E. machinist, house 11 Water
" John, farmer, house Foster, K. D.
" John A. house Johnson
" J. Martin, machinist, house Sutton n. Shawsheen river
" John N. machinist, house Second near Main
" Moses, farmer, house Berry near Middleton line
" Moses P. house Berry near Middleton line
" Putnam, farmer, house Moses do.
" William, emp. G. H. Tuttle, boards do.
Townsend William H. moulder, house 56 East Water
Tracey Michael, house Water
Trainor Annie, weaver, boards Mrs. Kate Kilburn
Trombley Ida P. dressmaker, house Joseph do.
" Joseph, stone mason, house Union near Marblehead
Trulan Catherine Mrs. (Hugh) house Marblehead

All Patent Medicines sold at bottom prices, by **Perkins, the Druggist.**

Tucker Charles W. house Mill
TUCKER EDGAR R. milk, house Rose Meadow Farm, Essex
" George, farmer and cider mfr. house off Johnson, F. D.
" William P. house Tucker
Tufts Eugene D. machinist, house 4 Water
" Jesse W. house Water
Turner Alfred, machinist, house School
Tuttle George H. farmer, house Andover near Lowell road
Twohey William J. carpenter, house Stevens near Pleasant
Tymon Bridget, domestic, house William A. Russell

U

UTSON WILLIAM H. wool sorter, boards Edwin Wright

W

WADLIN MELVIN T. overseer at Davis & Furber's, h. Maple av.
Wagner Atwood O. laborer, boards William H. Smith
" Jabez N. emp. Edward Adams, house Main opp. First
" Javey, house Stevens
Waite Fred W. supt. Stevens mill, N. A. house Court n. Osgood
Walker Margaret Mrs. house William R. Baxter
" Rudolphus W. pattern maker, house Maple av.
Wall Edward, spinner, house Eugene do.
" Eugene, laborer, house Main near Public Library
Wallwork Betsey Mrs. (Jonathan) house David W. do.
" Charles B. flagman B. & M. R. R. house Sutton n. Main
" David W. card setter, house Sutton
" Thomas W. clerk George Perkins, house David W. do.
Walshe Annie G. Mrs. house Main near First
Ward Charles E. machinist, house School
" William, house Phillips court near Pleasant
" William, Jr. machinist, house Railroad near Maple av.
Wardwell Franklin, house Salem
" Fred C. E. farmer, house George do.
" George, farmer, house Salem, K. D.
" Timothy O. house Osgood near Stevens
Warren Aaron R. clothing dealer, house Marblehead
WARREN FRANK A. clothing dealer, 187 Essex, Lawrence, house Marblehead
Waterhouse George H. watchman Davis & Furber, boards Charles J. Kelley
Waters Martin, emp. Stevens mill, boards John Wilton

Fine Confectionery, Stationery, Pocket Knives and Razors. **PERKINS, the DRUGGIST.**

Watson Solomon, machinist, boards Thomas P. Wills
Watts Eli H. moulder, house 8 Water
" John R. second hand Pacific mill, house Main near First
" V. B. machinist, house 8 Maple av.
Way Sarah E. Mrs. (George) house Court c. Pleasant
Weaver Howard W. farmer, house Salem, K. D.
Webber Gardner M. painter, boards Mrs. Ellen T. Morrissey
Webster Abbie Mrs. (John) house Pleasant near Elm
" Clara A. Mrs. (Thomas K.) house Joseph Robinson
" Daniel, teamster, house Stevens c. Salem
" Henry A. wool sorter, house 5 Suffolk
Weed Celeste, boards G. W. Berrian
Weekson Edward, carpenter, house rear 18 Beverly
Weil Anna Mrs. (Lewis) house Johnson

WEIL FRANK E., M. D. physician and surgeon, office and residence Main opp. Third, office hours 12.30 to 2 and 7 to 9 p. m.

" George L. counsellor at law, house Andover, C. D.
Welch Sarah, house Frank L. Bryant
Welsh John, iron and steel cutter, house First
" Thomas, house Water
Wentworth Thomas P. card setter Davis & Furber, h. 13 Pleasant
Wheeler Frank B. teamster, house Lake View Farm
White Henry, foreman spinning room Sutton mill, house Sutton near Sutton mill
" Samuel, house Henry do.
Whitehead Edward, spinner, house Sutton
" Squire, spinner, house Ashland c. Ferry
Whitman George H. teamster Standard Oil Co. h. 35 Marblehead
WHITNEY H. M. druggist, 297 Essex, Lawrence, house Stevens near Osgood
Whittaker William P. teamster, house Osgood near Andover
Whittier Hubert M. farmer, house Essex, P. D.
" Phineas W. machinist, house foot May

Physicians' Prescriptions and all Medicinal Compounds

Wilcox Charles, farmer, house Johnson, C. D.

WILCOX JOHN, horseshoer and carriage mfr. Andover, house Johnson
" Robert, emp. Sutton mill, house Sutton

Wild Walter H. Capt. house Andover, C. D.
Wilder Frank E. house Middlesex
Wiley John A. (Davis & Furber) house Elm c. Water
Williams George S. farmer, house off Andover n. Andover line
Willis David, moulder, house 50 East Water
Wills Thomas P. boarding house Pleasant, house do.
Wilson Abiel, house Andover corner Salem Turnpike
" George E. machine fitter Davis & Furber, house Main
" Orin L. painter, house Pleasant near Davis
Wilton George, spinner, house White Row
" George H. weaver, house George do.
" John, boarding house, house White Row
Winkley William T. loom fixer, house River View near the brook
Winning Andrew, emp. Stevens mill, house Mrs. Margaret do.
" Frederick, spinner, house Mrs. Margaret do.
" John, spinner, house Mrs. Margaret do.
" Margaret Mrs. (James) house Phillips court n. Pleasant
Wircox Jeannette Mrs. (John) house Sutton
Wise William N. house Pleasant
Wood Adam, stationary engineer, house 5 Beverly
" Ann Mrs. house Main opp. Bradstreet school house
Woodbody William, house River View
Woodhouse James, overseer carding room, North Andover mill, house Main near public library
" James, 2d, machinist, house 22 Pleasant
Woolley William, machinist, house 32 East Water
Wormald Mary Mrs. house 43 East Water
Wright Alice Mrs. (Thomas) house William Cunningham
" Edwin, machinist, house Pleasant near Davis
" Elijah, foreman at Davis & Furber's, h. Elm n. Water
" George L. (Davis & Furber) house Elm near Water
" Walter C. engineer at Sagehomme & Byers', h. 51 Main
Wrigley John, spinner, house Sutton

Y

YOUNG JAMES, machinist, house opp. 4 Pleasant
" Lila S. Mrs. house Mrs. Mary H. Sutton
" Oscar T. house Salem
Yox Frank, house Prospect

Prepared with care and accuracy. Perkins, the Druggist.

KENNELLY & SYLVESTER, 248 & 250 Essex St., Lawrence.

F. L. SARGENT,
BOARDING and BAITING STABLE.

Hacks furnished for Weddings, Parties or Funerals.

BARGES FOR ANY OCCASIONS.

PASSENGERS and Baggage Transferred to all parts of North Andover and vicinity.

SARGENT COURT, off Main Street.

North Andover Business Directory.

Agricultural Implements.

FULLER JOHN H. Elm near Water (see page 118)
HOLT T. A. & CO. Phillips square, C. D. (see page 103)
RICHARDSON J. W. Main (see page 116)

Auctioneer.

Holt Peter, Jr.

Band.

MECHANICS BRASS BAND, J. L. Downing leader

Baggage Transfer.

SARGENT F. L. Sargent court (see page 156)

Physicians' Prescriptions are guaranteed to be compounded from THE BEST QUALITY OF MEDICINE,

PIANOS AND ORGANS, 248 & 250 Essex Street, Lawrence.

Bakers.

COOPER EDWARD, 41 Main (dealer) (see page 115)
SANBORN JOHN F. Stonington (see page 110)
Currier A. P. (dealer) Water

Blacksmiths.

ADAMS EDWARD, Center District (see page 108)
ELLIS A. P. Railroad (see page 163)
Hinxman S. D. Sargent court
WILCOX JOHN, Andover, C. D. (see page 114)

Boarding Houses.

Dame Charles, Water
Holt Albert N. Prospect, C. D. (summer boarders)
Kilburn Kate Mrs. Main opp. school house
McCarthy Hannah Mrs. Water
MORRISSEY ELLEN T. MRS. Main (see page 116)
Perkins W. B. Mrs. 1 Pleasant (corporation)
Wills Thomas P. Pleasant
Wilton John, White Row

Books, Stationery, Periodicals, Etc.

Harris George L. Water

Boots, Shoes and Rubbers.

BROWN J. G. Water (see page 102)
FULLER JOHN H. Elm near Water (see page 118)
McNiff Thomas, Middlesex

Boot and Shoe Makers and Repairers.

Collina William, Water
Dunbar Martin, Water

Carpenters and Builders.

Costello Dennis J. Union
Currier Aaron A. Prescott
Daw Patrick P. Second
Rea William H. Osgood

ABSOLUTELY PURE, and IN STRICT ACCORDANCE with Physicians' orders, at **Perkins'.**

SHEET MUSIC, 248 & 250 Essex St., Lawrence.

Carriage Mfrs.

ADAMS EDWARD, Center District (see page 108)
ELLIS A. P. Railroad (see page 163)
Hinxman S. D. Sargent court
WILCOX JOHN, Andover, C. D. (see page 114)

Carriage Painters.

Hinxman S. D. Sargent court
McDONALD & HANNAFORD, C. D. (see page 118)

Cider Mfrs.

Foster Orrin
REYNOLDS J. E. & SON, Johnson (see page 117)
Tucker George, off Johnson

Cigars, Tobacco, Etc.
[See also Druggists and Grocers.]

Coal Dealers.

JACOBS J. Main (see page 116)
McKone Francis E. & Co. Water

Confectionery, Fruit, Etc.

Currier A. P. & Co. Water

Crockery, Glassware, Etc.

FULLER J. H. Elm (see page 118)
RICHARDSON J. W. Main (see page 116)

Depot Carriages.

SARGENT F. L. Sargent court (see page 156)

Dining Room.

MORRISSEY ELLEN T. MRS. Main (see page 116)

Perfumery, Toilet and Medicinal Soaps,

Tuning & Repairing Pianos at 248 & 250 Essex St., Lawrence.

Dressmakers.

Armitage M. & M. J. Main
Coughlin Nellie D.
FLEMING JULIA C. Main (see page 104)
Fuller Carrie R.
Grogan Annie A.
Lamere Mary H.
Trombly Ida P. Main

Drugs and Medicines.

PERKINS GEORGE H. Water (see underlines)
STEARNS C. S. Main (see front cover)

Dry and Fancy Goods.

Armitage M. & M. J. Main
BROWN J. G. Water (see page 102)
FULLER JOHN H. Elm near Water (see page 118)
HOLT T. A. & CO. Phillips square, C. D. (see page 103)
MAHONEY ELLEN MRS. East Water (see page 102)
McNiff Thomas, Middlesex

Expresses.

Josselyn's Express, G. C. Josselyn prop. office 25 Pleasant

Flour and Grain.

COOPER EDWARD, 41 Main (see page 115)
Currier A. P. & Co. Water
FULLER JOHN H. Elm near Water (see page 118)
HOLT T. A. & CO. Phillips square, C. D. (see page 103)
RICHARDSON J. W. Main (see page 116)

Grocers.

COOPER EDWARD, 41 Main (see page 115)
Currier A. P. & Co. Water
FULLER JOHN H. Elm near Water (see page 118)
HOLT T. A. & CO. Phillips square, C. D. (see page 103)
MAHONEY ELLEN MRS. East Water (see page 102)
McNiff Thomas, Sutton c. Main
RICHARDSON J. W. Main (see page 116)

Sponges, Chamois Skins. Perkins, the Druggist.

STRINGS of all kinds at 248 & 250 Essex St., Lawrence.

Hair Dressers.

Kelley Edward J. Water
Sharpe J. W. Main opp. public library

Harness Makers.

McDONALD & HANNAFORD, C. D. (see page 118)

Hay, Straw, Etc.

HOLT T. A. & CO. C. D. (see page 103)

Horseshoers.

ADAMS EDWARD, C. D. (see page 108)
Hinxman S. D. Sargent court
WILCOX JOHN, Andover, C. D. (see page 114)

Ice Dealers.

ADAMS EDWARD, C. D. (see page 108)
GREENWOOD FRANK M. Pond (see page 102)

Insurance.

COLBY EDMUND S. office Middlesex (see page 104)
Field H. W. Main
Morrissey John A. Water

Laundry Agents.

BROWN J. G. Water (see page 102)
Cheney A. P. Water
Harris G. L. Water

Lawyers.

Frye Newton P. Elm
Mahoney John P. S. East Water
Weil George L. Andover

Our assortment of TOOTH BRUSHES cannot be beat. **Perkins, the Druggist.**

BANJOS AND GUITARS at 248 & 250 Essex St., Lawrence.

Livery, Sale and Boarding Stables.

Cheney A. P. Water
Loring George B. Prospect
SARGENT F. L. Sargent court (see page 156)

Lumber Dealers.

JACOBS J. Main (see page 116)

Machinists.

Davis & Furber Machine Co. office Water c. Elm

Manufacturers.

Brown J. C. & Co. (curled hair and brush stock) office foot Suffolk
Campbell M. F. (asbestos toweling) Sutton
Davis & Furber Machine Co. (woolen machinery, mill shafting, etc.) office Water c. Elm
Glennie John, (soap) Lawrence street
North Andover Mill, (dress goods) Eben Sutton treas.
Sagehomme & Byers, (dress goods)
Stevens M. T. & Sons, (woolen goods) F. W. Waite supt.
The Sutton Mill, (ladies' dress goods and flannels) W. Sutton treas.

Masons and Contractors.

Driscoll & O'Brien, Salem Turnpike
Dunnils George W. off Main
Keniston Henry, Main near Merrimac
Trombly Joseph, Union

Meat and Provisions.

Barker G. L. Main
Meserve Charles E. Pleasant

Milk Dealers.

Doherty Patrick, First
Hughes Winfield S. Essex
Robinson Addison M. Stevens
TUCKER EDGAR R. Essex (see page 110)

Upon the Purity of Drugs and the reliability of our work we depend. **PERKINS, THE DRUGGIST.**

22

Pianos & Organs Tuned at 248 & 250 Essex St., Lawrence.

Mortgages.

COLBY EDMUND S. Middlesex (see page 104)

Music Teachers.

Butterworth Edward, (vocal) Main
DOWNING JOHN L. High (see page 104)
Lynch Harry, Second
Manning Harriet E. (piano-forte)
Marston Della, (piano-forte)
Saunders Lizzie, Elm

Nurse.

McCabe Sarah Mrs. Main near First

Oil Company.

Standard Oil Company of New York, Boston dept. D. W. Carney supt.

Painters and Paper Hangers.

Gould George, Osgood
Lowe John, Main opp. Second
REXTROW GEORGE, Church (see page 106)
Tattersall Joseph H. Second

Physicians.

MORRILL CHARLES P., M. D. office Elm (see page 142)
WEIL FRANK E., M. D. office Main (see page 154)

Plumber.

LEITCH JAMES W. Water (see page 114)

Real Estate.

COLBY EDMUND S. office Middlesex (see page 104)

Stoves, Ranges, Etc.

LEITCH JAMES W. Water (see page 114)

For Quality and Price PERKINS' Extract Jamaica Ginger leads them all. **PERKINS, THE DRUGGIST.**

LARGE STOCK PIANOS at 248 & 250 Essex St., Lawrence.

Teaming and Jobbing.

ADAMS EDWARD, C. D. (see page 108)
Bryant Frank L. Middlesex
Cheney A. P. Water

Tinsmith.

LEITCH JAMES W. Water (see page 114)

Variety Stores.

Cheney A. P. Water
Murphy Patrick P. Main
Schofield James Mrs. Main

Wheelwrights.

ADAMS EDWARD, C. D. (see page 108)
ELLIS A. P. Railroad (see page 163)
Hinxman S. D. Sargent court

Wood.

ADAMS EDWARD, C. D. (see page 108)

LATEST MUSIC at 248 & 250 Essex Street, Lawrence.

A. P. ELLIS,

——MANUFACTURER OF——

HEAVY CARTS AND WAGONS.

Repairing of all kinds.

Shop, Railroad Street, No. Andover.

If you want Patent Medicines at cut-rate prices, (guaranteed genuine,) go to **PERKINS, the Druggist.**

GREENE & WOODLIN,

—DEALERS IN—

DRY GOODS, GROCERIES,

Boots and Shoes,

CROCKERY, WOOD AND GLASS WARE, FLOUR, GRAIN, &C.

Wood of all kinds.

ANDOVER STREET,   BALLARD VALE.

Index to Andover Advertisers.

Abbott C. E., M. D.	29
American Express Co.	99
Andover National Bank	8
Andover Publishing Co., J. N. Cole prop.	86
Anderson & Bowman	99
Burke Patrick	20
Chandler G. W.	red page C
Chandler Marion R.	3
Chase H. F.	16
Chase O. P.	4
Cummings Brainard	inside last cover
Cummings Charles O.	25
Daly P. J.	red page C
Davis George E.	12
Farmer T. J.	20
Foster George W.	47
Georgi Theodore C.	3
Gilbert Charles H., M. D. S.	49
Gleason Frank E.	red page B
Greene & Woodlin	164
Gruber C. F.	18
Hannon P. J.	front cover
Harriman Thomas P.	4
Hayward H. M.	2

Hodges Amy M. Mrs.	12
Higgins W. H.	red page A
Holt T. A. & Co.	28
Joyce Patrick V.	2
Keeland John E.	2
Marland William	11
Mason C. B.	red page B
McLawlin Henry	inside last cover
Messer Frank H.	18
Muster Charles M.	26
O'Donnell Hugh	99
Poor William	26
Playdon John H.	100
Piddington George	7
Rhodes Thomas E.	7
Rowe E. J.	last cover
Sears J. C.	last cover
Scott C. W., M. D.	75
Shattuck C. H., M. D.	76
Sherry R. J.	100
Smith & Manning	28
Stickney & Howell	8
Trulan William F.	26
Tuttle B. B.	4
Tyer Rubber Co.	red page A
Valpey Bros.	87
Wakefield J. P.	12
Walsh Michael T.	5
White M. S.	last cover
Whiting John E.	12

SPARROW & FARNSWORTH,

· · Publishers of · ·

RESIDENT AND BUSINESS DIRECTORIES,

Shirley Village, Mass.

We can supply Directories of the following named Towns and Cities, at regular price, $1.00 per copy:

ANDOVER AND NORTH ANDOVER, MASS. (Combined.)
BELFAST AND CAMDEN, MAINE. (Combined.)
MILLBURY, MASS.   ROCHESTER (CITY), N. H.
WEYMOUTH, MASS.   QUINCY (CITY), MASS.
PLYMOUTH, MASS.   PALMER, MASS.
METHUEN, MASS.   WARE, MASS.

Many of the above named Directories contain Maps.

Index to North Andover Advertisers.

Adams Edward, blacksmith, wheelwright, ice, teaming, etc....... 108
Brown J. G. dry and fancy goods, boots, shoes, etc.............. 102
Colby Edmund S. insurance, real estate, mortgages............. 104
Cooper Edward, grocer... 115
Downing John L. instructor musical instruments............... 104
Ellis A. P. blacksmith and wheelwright....................... 163
Fleming Julia C. Miss, dressmaker............................ 104
Fuller John H. groceries, dry goods, etc..................... 118
Greenwood Frank M. ice....................................... 102
Holt T. A. & Co. general merchandise......................... 103
Jacobs J. coal and lumber.................................... 116
Leitch James W. stoves, ranges, plumbing, etc................ 114
Mahoney Ellen Mrs. groceries, etc............................ 102
McDonald & Hannaford, harness makers and carriage painters.... 118
Morrill Charles P., M. D. physician........................... 142
Morrissey Ellen T. Mrs. dining rooms......................... 116
Perkins George H. druggist............................... footlines
Rextrow George, painter and paper hanger..................... 106
Reynolds J. E. & Son, cider mfrs............................. 117
Richardson J. W. grocer...................................... 116
Sanborn John F. baker.. 110
Sargent Fred L. boarding and baiting stable.................. 156
Stearns C. S. druggist.................................. front cover
Tucker Edgar R. milk... 110
Weil Frank E., M. D. physician............................... 154
Wilcox John, blacksmith, wheelwright, etc.................... 114

POPULATION OF MASSACHUSETTS.

A star (*) indicates a shire town. Cities in boldface.

COUNTIES, CITIES AND TOWNS.	U. S. Census 1890.	COUNTIES, CITIES AND TOWNS.	U. S. Census 1890.	COUNTIES, CITIES AND TOWNS.	U. S. Census 1890.
BARNSTABLE.		Berkley	894	Rockport	4,087
Barnstable*	4,023	Dartmouth	3,122	Rowley	1,248
Bourne	1,442	Dighton	1,889	**Salem***	30,801
Brewster	1,003	Easton	4,493	Salisbury	1,316
Chatham	1,954	Fairhaven	2,919	Saugus	3,673
Dennis	2,899	**Fall River**	74,398	Swampscott	3,198
Eastham	602	Freetown	1,417	Topsfield	1,022
Falmouth	2,567	Mansfield	3,432	Wenham	886
Harwich	2,734	**New Bedford***	40,733	West Newbury	1,796
Mashpee	298	North Attleborough	6,727		
Orleans	1,219	Norton	1,785	Totals	299,995
Provincetown	4,642	Raynham	1,340		
Sandwich	1,819	Rehoboth	1,786	**FRANKLIN.**	
Truro	919	Seekonk	1,317	Ashfield	1,025
Wellfleet	1,291	Somerset	2,106	Bernardston	770
Yarmouth	1,760	Swansea	1,456	Buckland	1,570
		Taunton*	25,448	Charlemont	972
Totals	29,172	Westport	2,599	Colrain	1,671
				Conway	1,451
BERKSHIRE.		Totals	186,465	Deerfield	2,910
Adams	9,213			Erving	972
Alford	297	**DUKES.**		Gill	960
Becket	946	Chilmark	353	Greenfield*	5,252
Cheshire	1,308	Cottage City	1,080	Hawley	515
Clarksburg	884	Edgartown*	1,156	Heath	503
Dalton	2,885	Gay Head	139	Leverett	702
Egremont	845	Gosnold	135	Leyden	407
Florida	436	Tisbury	1,506	Monroe	282
Great Barrington	4,612			Montague	6,296
Hancock	506	Totals	4,369	New Salem	856
Hinsdale	1,739			Northfield	1,869
Lanesborough	1,018	**ESSEX.**		Orange	4,568
Lee	3,785	Amesbury	9,798	Rowe	541
Lenox	2,889	Andover	6,142	Shelburne	1,553
Monterey	495	Beverly	10,821	Shutesbury	453
Mount Washington	148	Boxford	865	Sunderland	663
New Ashford	125	Bradford	3,720	Warwick	565
New Marlborough	1,305	Danvers	7,454	Wendell	505
North Adams	16,074	Essex	1,713	Whately	779
Otis	583	Georgetown	2,117		
Peru	305	**Gloucester**	24,651	Totals	38,610
Pittsfield*	17,281	Groveland	2,191		
Richmond	796	Hamilton	961	**HAMPDEN.**	
Sandisfield	807	**Haverhill**	27,412	Agawam	2,352
Savoy	569	Ipswich	4,439	Blandford	871
Sheffield	1,954	**Lawrence***	44,654	Brimfield	1,096
Stockbridge	2,132	**Lynn**	55,727	Chester	1,295
Tyringham	412	Lynnfield	787	**Chicopee**	14,050
Washington	434	Manchester	1,789	Granville	1,061
West Stockbridge	1,492	Marblehead	8,202	Hampden	831
Williamstown	4,221	Merrimac	2,633	Holland	201
Windsor	612	Methuen	4,814	**Holyoke**	35,637
		Middleton	924	Longmeadow	2,163
Totals	81,108	Nahant	880	Ludlow	1,939
		Newbury	1,427	Monson	3,650
BRISTOL.		**Newburyport***	13,947	Montgomery	266
Acushnet	1,027	North Andover	3,742	Palmer	6,520
Attleborough	7,577	Peabody	10,158	Russell	879

COUNTIES, CITIES AND TOWNS.	U. S. Census 1890.	COUNTIES, CITIES AND TOWNS.	U. S. Census 1890.	COUNTIES, CITIES AND TOWNS.	U. S. Census 1890.
Southwick	914	Stoneham	6,155	Wareham	3,451
Springfield*	44,179	Stow	903	West Bridgewater	1,917
Tolland	393	Sudbury	1,197	Whitman	4,441
Wales	700	Tewksbury	2,515		
Westfield	9,805	Townsend	1,750	Totals	92,700
West Springfield	5,077	Tyngsborough	662		
Wilbraham	1,914	Wakefield	6,982	SUFFOLK.	
		Waltham	18,707	Boston*	448,477
Totals	135,713	Watertown	7,073	Chelsea	27,909
HAMPSHIRE.		Wayland	2,060	Revere	5,668
Amherst	4,512	Westford	2,250	Winthrop	2,726
Belchertown	2,120	Weston	1,664		
Chesterfield	609	Wilmington	1,313	Totals	484,780
Cummington	787	Winchester	4,861		
Easthampton	4,395	Woburn	13,499	WORCESTER.	
Enfield	902			Ashburnham	2,074
Goshen	297	Totals	431,167	Athol	6,319
Granby	725			Auburn	1,532
Greenwich	526	NANTUCKET.		Barre	2,239
Hadley	1,669	Nantucket*	3,268	Berlin	854
Hatfield	1,246			Blackstone	6,138
Huntington	1,285	NORFOLK.		Bolton	827
Middlefield	455	Avon	1,284	Boylston	770
Northampton*	14,990	Bellingham	1,234	Brookfield	3,352
Pelham	466	Braintree	4,848	Charlton	1,847
Plainfield	435	Brookline	12,103	Clinton	10,424
Prescott	376	Canton	4,538	Dana	700
Southampton	1,017	Cohasset	2,448	Douglas	1,908
South Hadley	4,261	Dedham*	7,123	Dudley	2,944
Ware	7,329	Dover	727	Fitchburg*	22,037
Westhampton	477	Foxborough	2,953	Gardner	8,424
Williamsburg	2,057	Franklin	4,831	Grafton	5,002
Worthington	714	Holbrook	2,474	Hardwick	2,922
		Hyde Park	10,193	Harvard	1,095
Totals	51,859	Medfield	1,453	Holden	2,623
MIDDLESEX.		Medway	2,965	Hopedale	1,176
Acton	1,897	Millis	786	Hubbardston	1,346
Arlington	5,629	Milton	4,278	Lancaster	2,201
Ashby	825	Needham	3,035	Leicester	3,120
Ashland	2,532	Norfolk	913	Leominster	7,269
Ayer	2,148	Norwood	3,733	Lunenburg	1,146
Bedford	1,092	Quincy	16,723	Mendon	919
Belmont	2,098	Randolph	3,946	Milford	8,760
Billerica	2,380	Sharon	1,534	Millbury	4,428
Boxborough	325	Stoughton	4,852	New Braintree	573
Burlington	617	Walpole	2,604	Northborough	1,452
Cambridge*	70,028	Wellesley	3,600	Northbridge	4,603
Carlisle	451	Weymouth	10,866	North Brookfield	3,871
Chelmsford	2,695	Wrentham	2,598	Oakham	738
Concord	4,427			Oxford	2,616
Dracut	1,996	Totals	118,950	Paxton	445
Dunstable	416			Petersham	1,050
Everett	11,068	PLYMOUTH.		Phillipston	502
Framingham	9,239	Abington	4,260	Princeton	982
Groton	2,057	Bridgewater	4,249	Royalston	1,030
Holliston	2,619	Brockton	27,294	Rutland	980
Hopkinton	4,088	Carver	994	Shrewsbury	1,449
Hudson	4,670	Duxbury	1,908	Southborough	2,114
Lexington	3,197	East Bridgewater	2,911	Southbridge	7,655
Lincoln	987	Halifax	562	Spencer	8,747
Littleton	1,025	Hanover	2,093	Sterling	1,244
Lowell*	77,696	Hanson	1,267	Sturbridge	2,074
Malden	23,031	Hingham	4,564	Sutton	3,180
Marlborough	13,805	Hull	989	Templeton	2,999
Maynard	2,700	Kingston	1,659	Upton	1,278
Medford	11,079	Lakeville	935	Uxbridge	3,408
Melrose	8,519	Marion	871	Warren	4,681
Natick	9,118	Marshfield	1,713	Webster	7,031
Newton	24,379	Mattapoisett	1,148	Westborough	5,195
North Reading	874	Middleborough	6,065	West Boylston	3,019
Pepperell	3,127	Norwell	1,625	West Brookfield	1,592
Reading	4,088	Pembroke	1,320	Westminster	1,688
Sherborn	1,281	Plymouth*	7,314	Winchendon	4,390
Shirley	1,101	Plympton	597	Worcester*	84,655
Somerville	40,152	Rochester	1,012		
		Rockland	5,213	Totals	280,787
		Scituate	2,318		

Total Population of the State, 2,238,943.

BRAINARD CUMMINGS,
CONTRACTOR and BUILDER.

Plans & Specifications

Furnished for the erection of

BUILDINGS OF ANY SIZE OR STYLE.

BUILDING ✠ LUMBER

Constantly on hand, or furnished at short notice.

ALL JOBBING WILL RECEIVE PROMPT ATTENTION.

Shop, Park Street, Andover.

HENRY McLAWLIN,
—DEALER IN—

HARDWARE, CUTLERY,

Agricultural Implements,

CORDAGE, ✲ CARPENTERS' ✲ TOOLS,

Paints, Oils, Brushes,

WINDOW GLASS, &C.

❧ AKRON ✲ DRAIN ✲ PIPE, ☙

And a full line of

SPORTING ✲ GOODS.

Main Street, Andover, Mass.

AND CHEMICALS AT E. M. WHITNEY & CO.'S, LAWRENCE.

M. E. WHITE,
MASON and CONTRACTOR.

Special attention given to
SETTING FIREPLACES AND TILING.

Kalsomining, ✢ Whitening ✢ and ✢ Tinting.

OFFICE, ESSEX STREET, ANDOVER, MASS.

J. E. ——,
BAKER BUILDING, MAIN STREET, ANDOVER.

Carries a ———

Boots ——— and Rubbers

in the leading styles.

THE HYGIENIC FELT INNERSOLE SHOE

a specialty. A non-conductor of heat and cold.
Try a pair, with a bottle of
Sabine's Fine Oil Shoe Polish.

E. J. ROWE,

WALL PAPERS

—AND—

Interior Decorations.

FRESCO PAINTING A SPECIALTY.

OFFICE, - POST-OFFICE AVENUE.

READ OUR ADVERTISEMENT ON CARD INSET CAREFULLY.

H. M. WHITNEY & CO., Lawrence.

READ THE FIRST CARD INSET CAREFULLY.

This book is a preservation photocopy.
It is made in compliance with copyright law
and produced on acid-free archival
60# book weight paper
which meets the requirements of
ANSI/NISO Z39.48-1992 (permanence of paper)

Preservation photocopying and binding
by
Acme Bookbinding
Charlestown, Massachusetts

2001

www.ingramcontent.com/pod-product-compliance
Lightning Source LLC
Chambersburg PA
CBHW020921230426
43666CB00008B/1520